Joke Soup

Joke Soup

1,217

of the
Funniest Jokes
from the Best Comedians

edited by

Judy Brown

**Andrews McMeel
Publishing**

Kansas City

www.andrewsmcmeel.com

99 00 01 02 RDH 10 9 8 7 6 5 4

Library of Congress Cataloging-in-Publication Data

Brown, Judy.
   Joke soup : 1,217 of the funniest jokes from the best comedians / Judy Brown.
      p.   cm.
   ISBN 0-8362-6754-0 (pbk. : alk. paper)
   1. American wit and humor. I. Title.
PN6162.B737 1998
818'.540208--dc21   98-27463
                                                                      CIP

---- **ATTENTION: SCHOOLS AND BUSINESSES** ----

Andrews McMeel books are available at quantity discounts with bulk purchase for educational, business, or sales promotional use. For information, please write to: Special Sales Department, Andrews McMeel Publishing, 4520 Main Street, Kansas City, Missouri 64111.

Preface

I come from a comedy-loving family. Good-byes at Brown family gatherings were both pro-tracted and entertaining. They started with a full stop at the front door for one remembered funny story, the another dead stop in the middle of the sidewalk for yet another anecdote—or two, or four—and finally the car door was opened and leaned upon for maybe forty-five minutes for still more comebacks, asides—whatever.

And although they themselves practiced lengthy storytelling, my parents couldn't help but admire and enjoy those who worked professionally in one-liners, and who could somehow restrain themselves to a mere six minutes on Johnny Carson. They also loved those who worked in that fine half inch of ivory, set-up and punchline—in other words, stand-up comedians.

I caught the bug too—and early. I remember my grandparents lifting me out of my crib at 11:30 P.M. in order to indulge my precocious predilection for *The Tonight Show.* And for over a dozen years, I've been able to indulge myself professionally as a comedy critic for the *LA Weekly*.

The collection of jokes in *Joke Soup* spans, if

not comprehensively, almost a half century of American stand-up comedy, from the old-style jokey jokes of Henny Youngman to the ground-breaking comedians of my parents' generation, like Lenny Bruce and Dick Gregory, who helped transform comedy to a more conversational, confrontational, running-joke social commentary; and from comedians like Roseanne and Jerry Seinfeld, who helped rethink the sitcom, to alternative comedians like Janeane Garafola, who are deconstructing comedy and reconstructing it postmodernly.

I've also included a generous helping of material from working professional comedians and the promising, freshly minted funny people whose names may not be familiar to you. Yet. These are the talented pool from whom the next generation of comedy stars will come, and who will have a hand in creating next season's, next year's, and some of the next millennium's funny movies, television shows, and interactive laughs. I don't know about you, but I'm looking forward to slapstick holograms.

Acknowledgments

I've had a lot of fun following this pop culture art form, and first and foremost, I'd like to thank all the comedians who have made me laugh. I'd also like to acknowledge those publicists, comedy club owners, managers, executives, and agents who help those funny people ship the laughter out to us. Most especially, I'd like to thank Rick Messina and the rest of the talent at Messina Baker; Budd Friedman and all his jolly crew at the Improv; Bob Zmuda at Comic Relief; Mara Makalian and Suzanne Baum at HBO; my assistant, Jeannie Dietz (a comedy groupie in the best sense of the term); Elaine Tallas Cordone and the gang at the Ice House; Mike Lacy and family at the Comedy & Magic Club; Jeff Abraham, Michelle Marx, Jan Frasier, Monique Moss, Bob Read, and the HBO Workspace; First Circle Management; Sally Straub; Omnipop; the (other) Judi Brown Management; Lapides Entertainment; Strauss McGarr; Steve Hewitt of Showtime; Judy Pastore, formerly of Showtime; and those folks at Comedy Central who provide such fine entertainment at basic cable rates.

I'd also like to thank my hard-working agent, Carol Bidnick; Jean Zevnik and Christine Schillig

Acknowledgments

of Andrews McMeel Publishing for their editorial discrimination and incredible patience; and Cathryn Michon and Maria Hjelm for their help and encouragement and that nice lunch at Red.

And last but not least, I'd like to thank my family, who have put up with a lot of funny business from me. This includes my father, from whom I guess I inherited that sense-of-humor gene, and my brother, who I still think is one of the funniest people on the planet—although he insists on maintaining his amateur standing.

abcd

Abortion

I say to this dude with a "Stop Abortion" picket sign, "I have the answer to abortion—shoot your dick. Take that tired piece of meat down to the ASPCA and let 'em put it to sleep."

— *Whoopi Goldberg*

I'm getting an abortion. I don't need one, but I feel that as an American I should exercise that right before it gets taken away.

— *Betsy Salkind*

Accident

I spilled spot remover on my dog—now he's gone.

— *Steven Wright*

Do you think anyone's ever bitten their tongue, and then decided to eat the rest?

— *Drake Sather*

Affirmative Action

How come the white male politicians who vote against affirmative action are always so willing to accept a handicap on the golf course?

— *Paul Krassner*

Africa

I went to Africa. Now I know how white people feel in America—relaxed. 'Cause you hear a police car coming, you know it ain't coming after *your* ass.

— *Richard Pryor*

Age

Fuck the Gen Xers. It's their diapers that are clogging up the landfill.

— *Betsy Salkind*

I think I look good for forty-two. However, my skin is starting to lose its elasticity. I took a nap on a corduroy bedspread. It took six hours for the lines to come out of my face.

— *Cathy Ladman*

I turned thirty, and suddenly I was at that point in your life where you want to eat Fruity Pebbles. But you're concerned about the fiber content.

— *Paul Provenza*

I'm getting older and I'm thinking about having my eggs frozen. Well, just the egg whites. I'm trying to cut back on my cholesterol.

— *Brenda Pontiff*

You know you're getting older when the first thing you do after you're done eating is look for a place to lie down.

— *Louie Anderson*

When I hit my thirties I found there's less hair on my head and more in my ears.

— *Robert Wuhl*

Old is always fifteen years from now.

— *Bill Cosby*

You can teach an old dog new tricks, you just don't want to watch the dog doing them.

— *Bill Cosby*

At my age, I'm lucky to get an erection. I'd be happy if a flag came out with a sign that said, "Hey, thanks for the opportunity."

— *Richard Lewis*

I can't wait till I get Alzheimer's—new pussy every night!

— *Bobby Slayton*

If you're less than ten years old you're so excited about aging you think in fractions. "How old are you?" "Six and a half!" You're never thirty-six and a half. Then a strange thing happens. If you make it over 100 you become a kid again: "104. And a half!"

— *Larry Miller*

There's one advantage to being 102. No peer pressure.

— *Dennis Wolfberg*

Ever get stuck walking behind old people in a crowd? No matter how hard you try you can't get around them. Then out of nowhere, they just stop, like their batteries went dead. It's like they have a sixth sense about getting in people's way. They should be guarding Jordan.

— *Drew Carey*

Alcohol

Is it bad when you refer to all alcohol as Pain Go Bye-Bye Juice?

— *Patton Oswalt*

If you enjoy your alcohol, remember this: If you put your old, rotten, used-up liver under your pillow, the Beer Fairy will leave you a keg.

— *Paul F. Tomkins*

I had to stop drinking, man. I got tired of waking up in my car driving ninety.

— *Richard Pryor*

My dad's life was a bender—mine's the hangover.

— *Bob Odenkirk*

I don't need to drink to have a good time—I need to drink to stop the voices in my head.

— *Dave Attell*

Alcohol kills brain cells. We take the only organ in our body that won't grow back and we kill it for fun.

— *Cary Odes*

I can't think of anything worse after a night of drinking than waking up next to someone and not being able to remember their name, or how you met, or why they're dead.

— *Laura Kightlinger*

Drive-through liquor stores, that's almost a good idea. Just the thing for that drunk driver who's constantly on the go. "Hey, no time to go to a real bar, I've got places to go, people to hit."

— *Drew Carey*

Don't drink and drive. Instead, the next time you get too drunk to drive, walk into a local Dominos and order a pizza. Then when they go to deliver it, ask for a ride home.

— *Todd Glass*

There are two groups of people in the world now. Those that get pathetically drunk in public—and the rest of us poor bastards who are expected to drive these pinheads home.

— *Dennis Miller*

If you get drunk, don't call a cab. That could cost you $20 or $40 or $50. Do what I do, call a tow truck. It might cost a little more, but your car will be there when you wake up.

— Jeffrey Jena

I wouldn't stop drinking till the bartender said, "We got no more fucking liquor! Take your ass home, pal."

— Richard Pryor

I can't hold my liquor in the winter. I'm pretty sure it's the mittens.

— Jonathan Katz

I'm an alcoholic, and I'm also out of shape. So I just joined a twelve-step aerobics group.

— Peter Spruyt

You have a baby, you have to clean up your act. You can't come in drunk and go, "Hey, here's a little switch, Daddy's going to throw up on *you*."

— Robin Williams

It's been over five years since I had a drink. I kind of miss sex.

— Tracy Smith

I think tobacco and alcohol warnings are too general. They should be more to the point: "People who smoke will eventually cough up brown pieces of lung." And "Warning! Alcohol will turn you into the same asshole your father was."

— *George Carlin*

Alone

I have come to realize that we are all truly on our own. Today, my wife yelled, "What do you want from me? I made you a bowl of cereal."

— *Paul Alexander*

Remember, we're all in this alone.

— *Lily Tomlin*

I like to live alone, you never have to clean up. I find things in the refrigerator, I figure out what they used to be.

— *Elayne Boosler*

Ambition

I have a list I made when I was twelve of things I
wanted to do before I die. Omigod. How embarrassing. No. 1: Touch a boobie.

— *Drew Carey*

America

People in other countries, they all want to come to
America. They say, "You can eat twenty-four hours a
day in America." I say yeah, they're right. If you
have some money or a pistol, you can get something
to eat.

— *Richard Pryor*

The average American attention span is that of a fer-
ret on a double espresso.

— *Dennis Miller*

On the pioneers: That was very important, the
wagon. Just as important as the wheels are today.
'Cause if the wagon broke down and you were too
dumb or lazy to fix it, that's where you stayed. You
don't think people headed out for Tulsa, do you? You

know, everywhere you see a nice big spread in America, they got two broken wheels outside.

— *Gallagher*

On the American colonists: They say, "We discovered new lands and territories." Hey, if you believe that, I can go to court and say, "Your honor, I was exploring some fire escapes and discovered this man's apartment. I planted my flag in his living room and now all his stuff is mine. Him and his wife came home—I had to shoot them, they were savages!"

— *Warren Hutcherson*

I don't believe there's any problem in this country, no matter how tough it is, that Americans, when they roll up their sleeves, can't completely ignore.

— *George Carlin*

Is intelligence a liability nowadays? I think we can answer that with one word: *Duh.* America's never been what you would call highbrow, but these days it seems our collective cranial ridge is sloping like the shoulders of the bar boy at the Kennedy compound.

— *Dennis Miller*

The people with brown skins were here first. The rest of you are lucky that the Indians didn't ask Columbus for his Green Card.

— *Charlie Hill*

Traditional American values: Genocide, aggression, conformity, emotional repression, hypocrisy, and the worship of comfort and consumer goods.

— *George Carlin*

Amusement Park

I don't understand people who go to amusement parks. I spend most of my time trying *not* to be nauseous and dizzy. "Excuse me, could you strap me in upside down? I'd like to be as sick as humanly possible. I feel great today, I think I'll go down to Funland and snap my neck on the back of a ride. Honey, let's bring the kids, I want to give them a spinal cord injury for Christmas."

— *Dom Irrera*

The Universal Studios ride Twister simulates the destructive forces of a twister so realistically that it was immediately surrounded by five trailer parks.

— *Craig Kilborn*

Animals

Animals may be our friends, but they won't pick you up at the airport.

— *Bobcat Goldthwait*

I find that ducks' opinion of me is greatly influenced by whether or not I have bread.

— *Mitch Hedberg*

If lobsters looked like puppies, people could never drop them in boiling water while they're still alive. But instead, they look like science fiction monsters, so it's okay. Restaurants that allow patrons to select live lobsters from a tank should be made to paint names on their shells: "Happy," "Baby Doll," "Junior." I defy anyone to drop a living thing called "Happy" in boiling water.

— *George Carlin*

When I was growing up, we had a petting zoo, and well, we had two sections. We had a petting zoo, and then we had a heavy petting zoo. For people who really liked the animals a lot.

— *Ellen DeGeneres*

To me, the most blatant example of cruelty to animals is the rotisserie. It's just a really morbid Ferris wheel for chickens.

— *Mitch Hedberg*

They do a lot of animal testing in the cosmetics industry, maybe they should brag about it in their commercials. "Aquanet hair spray, if it can blind a spider monkey, it can make your hair look luscious." Or "Gillette, because 4,000 bald squirrels can't be wrong."

— *Vernon Chapman*

Dolphin-safe tuna, that's great if you're a dolphin. What if you're a tuna? Somewhere there's a tuna flopping around a ship going, "What about me? I'm not cute enough for you?"

— *Drew Carey*

Stuffed deer heads on walls are bad enough, but it's worse when you see them wearing dark glasses, having streamers around their necks, and a hat on their antlers. Because then you know they were enjoying themselves at a party when they were shot.

— *Ellen DeGeneres*

One thing sickens me about animals being on stage entertaining. The trainer will have the animals jumping through fire doing flips, sitting up . . . you know, really putting on a show. And then, the trainer takes a bow! Every time I see an animal that attacks a trainer on one of those TV specials, I think, "Well, no wonder. The Supremes should've done something like that to Diana Ross a long time ago."

— *Drew Carey*

Yesterday on the ice rink at Rockefeller Center, two women protesting the wearing of fur skated nude. Nude ice skating—I'm thinking to myself, man, this is just the thing to get Tonya Harding out of retirement.

— *David Letterman*

I saw this water-safety manual that actually says if a shark attacks, you should poke it in the eyes! Who wrote that, the Three Stooges?

— *Larry Reeb*

As yet there have been no deaths attributed to the killer bees. However, two bees were caught this week planning a murder.

— *Dennis Miller*

Anthropology

We're not descended here from a bunch of fat cave people who got eaten by the dinosaurs. We're all descended from the little bitty quick suckers who got back to the cave.

— *Gallagher*

Arms Control

Do you realize why we have arms control now? It's because we're broke, and the Russians are broke. Before arms control, we were like two junkies arguing over a plastic spoon.

— *Robin Williams*

Art

If a painting can be forged well enough to fool experts, why is the original so valuable?

— *George Carlin*

I think the most memorable experience I had in France was visiting the cathedral at Chartres. It's a 400-year-old cathedral—beautiful stained glass, and it's a very,

very moving experience, and as I was writing my
name on it with a can of spray paint . . .

— *Steve Martin*

Fifty something million dollars for a Van Gogh. You
know, if there is an afterlife, and if Vincent is up there
watching, he's chopping off the other ear, going, "Son
of a bitch! When I was alive I couldn't sell dick!"

— *Paul Rodriguez*

Critics say that Andy Warhol's famous portraits of
Campbell's soup cans were a brilliant satire of culture, in much the same way Campbell's soup is a brilliant satire of food.

— *Craig Kilborn*

Astronomy

I've been getting into astronomy, so I installed a
skylight. The people who live above me are furious.

— *Steven Wright*

Attitude

The chip on my shoulder's a little heavy. I have back problems now.

— *Janeane Garofalo*

I had a stick of Carefree gum, but it didn't work. I felt pretty good while I was blowin' that bubble, but as soon as the gum lost its flavor, I went back to pondering my mortality.

— *Mitch Hedberg*

No matter how cynical you get, it's impossible to keep up.

— *Lily Tomlin*

I was a born pessimist. My first words were, "My bottle is half empty."

— *Lacie Harmon*

I'm not a pessimist: I like to think of myself as an optimist with a reality chaser. I know the glass is half full. I just want to know who the hell's been drinking out of it, and do I have to pay full price?

— *Bob Zany*

Do you feel that excitement of being a woman in the nineties? Maybe it's just static cling.

— *Rhonda Hansome*

If a man smiles all the time he's probably selling something that doesn't work.

— *George Carlin*

Baby

I think God made babies cute so we don't eat them.

— *Robin Williams*

I still can't believe that people I know, my peers, are making babies. I'm too lazy to make a salad.

— *Hellura Lyle*

My sister was in labor for thirty-six hours. Ow. She got wheeled out of delivery, looked at me, and said, "Adopt."

— *Caroline Rhea*

We have a baby now at my house . . . all day long. And all night long. I wonder why they say you have a baby? The baby has you.

— *Gallagher*

A lucky woman in Iowa delivered seven babies. Ooh, that is not a delivery—that, my friends, is a shipment! You know, if you think about it, for parents it's a dream—or a nightmare, I guess. Doesn't make any difference, either way they're never going to sleep again.

— *David Letterman*

The baby is great. My wife and I have just started potty training. Which I think is important, because when we wanna potty-train the baby we should set an example.

— *Howie Mandel*

I can't decide if I want a baby. And my friends who have kids don't make very good salesmen. They're like, "Oh you learn all this great stuff, like how to survive on two hours' sleep." If I want to learn that I'll just become a political prisoner or something.

— *Cathryn Michon*

Women forty-nine years old are having their first child. Forty-nine! I couldn't think of a better way to spend my golden years. What's the advantage of having a kid at forty-nine? So you can both be in diapers at the same time?

— *Sue Kolinsky*

This is exciting. A woman recently had a baby from an embryo that had been frozen for seven years. She said, "I had no idea if I was having a little boy, a little girl—or fish sticks."

— *Conan O'Brien*

As far as baby-sitting tips go, I recommend a few quick questions to the parents when you want to get out early. Like, "Is it all right for the baby to have . . . bleach?"

— *Jake Johannsen*

Our baby won't suck on her thumb. She prefers her two middle fingers. Which makes her look like a little, tiny bulimic. I knew she was going to be a supermodel.

— *Vance Sanders*

Babies in strollers frighten me. They're never happy. Always screaming and drooling, scrunched up in that little chair. They look like little angry Larry Flynts.

— *Matt Weinhold*

Bachelor Party

It was one of those bachelor parties where all the married men had to meet at the end and decide about what to say we did. "We got in a fight with some guys and that's how our underwear got ripped. They ripped our underwear, and smelled good. Jimmy, you fell and your nipple got pierced."

— *Ray Romano*

Banking

The lady at the bank asked, "What do you want on your checks—wildlife, scenery?" I said, "I want a picture of a big, thick-necked guy on my checks. A bouncer—that's what my checks are going to be."

— *Bob Kubota*

I went to the bank and went over my savings. I found out I have all the money that I'll ever need. If I die tomorrow.

— *Henny Youngman*

The banks have a new image. Now you have "a friend." Your friendly banker. If the banks are so friendly, how come they chain down the pens?

— *Alan King*

Barbie

Barbie is getting a bigger waist and a smaller chest. Not surprisingly, earlier today Ken announced he wants to start seeing other dolls.

— *David Letterman*

A toy company is releasing Teacher Barbie this week. Apparently, it's like Malibu Barbie—only she can't afford the Corvette.

— *Stephanie Miller*

Feminists miss the big picture. They want us to be concerned about the fact that Barbie, if she were a real woman, would have no internal organs because her waist is too small. I say, Barbie's got nothing to complain about in the missing organ department, compared to Ken.

— *Cathryn Michon*

Beauty

The Miss America pageant is very pro-education. They give the winner a full college scholarship. Which is just what Harvard needs, more bulimics who play the ukulele.

— *Sheila Wenz*

I can't believe we still have the Miss America pageant. This is America! Where we're not supposed to judge people based on how they look; we're supposed to judge people based on how much money they make.

— *Heidi Joyce*

At the always hilarious Miss USA Pageant, Miss Massachusetts was crowned winner and vowed to fight "drugs and violence" —with her rock-hard pecs, I guess.

— *Craig Kilborn*

All God's children are not beautiful. Most of God's children are, in fact, barely presentable.

— *Fran Liebowitz*

There's no leeway for a woman's looks. You never see a man walking down the street with a woman who has a little pot belly and a bald spot.

— *Elayne Boosler*

Biological Clock

My girlfriend is at that stage where her biological clock is telling her it's time for her to be making me feel guilty and immature.

— *Kevin Hench*

Birth

I don't get no respect. When I was born, the doctor smacked my mother.

— *Rodney Dangerfield*

When I was born, I weighed three pounds four ounces. It's not that I was premature. It's just that when my older brother was born he left the womb a complete and total mess. I spent the first three months of my gestation just vacuuming.

— *Jon Stewart*

If you don't yell during labor, you're a fool. I screamed. Oh, how I screamed. And that was just during the conception.

— *Joan Rivers*

People are giving birth underwater now. They say it's less traumatic for the baby because it's in water. But certainly more traumatic for the other people in the pool.

— *Elayne Boosler*

When the doctor asked me if I wanted a bikini cut for my cesarean section, I said, "No! A bikini and a wine cooler is why I'm laying up here now."

— *Kim Tavares*

You take Lamaze classes. I went. It was a total waste of time. Ain't nobody going to breathe a baby out. There's going to be a fight.

— *Sinbad*

It's been over ten years since my wife and I pounded out our daughter. That's kind of an extremely sensitive way to say we had a child. It was a blessed event, a wonderful, miraculous thing. But it also showed me what a self-centered dick I am. The doctor says, "Mr. Goldthwait, we're going to have to perform a C-section." Instead of going, "Oh, my God, I hope everything's okay," I went, "Oh, great, I went to Lamaze for nothing."

— *Bobcat Goldthwait*

Everyone I know is having a baby and I'm childless. They all have these incredible stories and everything I do in comparison seems inconsequential. They say, "Well I was in labor for eleven hundred hours. I had the baby out in the woods. And now I'm back at work full time and I'm breast feeding." I'm like, "I bought a new skirt."

— *Caroline Rhea*

The Vatican came down with a new ruling: no surrogate mothers. Good thing they didn't make this rule before Jesus was born.

— *Elayne Boosler*

She's screaming like crazy . . . You have this myth you're sharing the birth experience. Unless you're circumcising yourself with a chain saw, I don't think so. Unless you're opening an umbrella up your ass, I don't think so!

— *Robin Williams*

My wife—God bless her—was in labor for thirty-two hours. And I was faithful to her the entire time.

— *Jonathan Katz*

Lamaze expects the husband—me—to be there, so that I can witness this festivity. I did not want to be there. This was remarkably painful for my wife. There was nothing my presence could really do to relieve her pain. In other words, I didn't see why my evening should be ruined too.

— *Dennis Wolfberg*

I want to have children, but my friends scare me. One of my friends told me she was in labor for thirty-six hours. I don't even want to do anything that feels good for thirty-six hours.

— *Rita Rudner*

The doctor took my baby out of my wife's stomach. Then he turned to me and asked, "Mr. Goldthwait, would you like to cut the cord?" And I said, "Isn't there anyone more qualified?"

— *Bobcat Goldthwait*

My baby, "Hesitation Klein," took twenty hours of labor to come out. They used a plunger at the end.

— *Robert Klein*

My wife showed courage throughout the ordeal of giving birth. Until the end, when she whispered through her clenched teeth, "I want you to come close to me now, honey—so I can grab your testicles and you can understand the pain I'm going through."

— *Don Ware*

In this day and age women can have kids for other women through surrogate motherhood. Is this the ultimate favor or what? I think I'm a good friend. I'll help you move. Okay. But whatever comes out of me after nine months, I'm keeping. I don't care if it's a shoe.

— *Sue Kolinsky*

Birth Control

In a test program, forty drugstores in Washington State will be dispensing morning-after birth control pills without prescription. In fact, men can buy them in special gift packs with cards that say, "Thanks, maybe I'll call you sometime."

— *Jay Leno*

I was dating a control freak. He insisted that *he* take the birth control pills.

— *Wendy Liebman*

A birth control pill for men, that's fair. It makes more sense to take the bullets out of the gun than to wear a bulletproof vest.

— *Greg Travis*

I'm Catholic. My mother and I were unpacking and she found my diaphragm. I had to tell her it was a bathing cap for my cat.

— *Lizz Winstead*

I practice birth control, which is being around my sister's children. You want to run right out and ovulate after you play with them for five minutes.

— *Brett Butler*

Black

I was a Negro for twenty-three years; I gave that shit up— no room for advancement.

— *Richard Pryor*

Black unemployment is up 50 percent of the time. That's not a bad thing, because the last time we were fully employed, we didn't have benefits like freedom.

— *Shang*

I was constantly being harassed by retailers and security guards, and I didn't understand why. Then I was informed by my friends that when I shop, I flaunt my melanin.

— *Hellura Lyle*

We come from the first people on Earth. We the first people that had thought, "Where the fuck am I, and how do you get to Detroit?"

— *Richard Pryor*

Blondes

Blondes have more fun, don't they? They must. How many brunettes do you see walking down the street with blond roots?

— *Rita Rudner*

Books

The book *It:* I just couldn't believe Stephen King wrote this. "Honey! there's a pronoun in the basement! There's a pronoun in the basement!"

— *Richard Lewis*

I just got out of the hospital. I was in a speed-reading accident. I hit a bookmark.

— *Steven Wright*

Why pay a dollar for a bookmark? Use the dollar as a bookmark.

— *Fred Stoller*

I honestly believe there is absolutely nothing like going to bed with a good book. Or a friend who's read one.

— *Phyllis Diller*

I have a new book coming out. It's one of those self-help deals; it's called *How to Get Along with Everyone.* I wrote it with this other asshole.

— *Steve Martin*

Boyfriend

Boyfriend. This is such a weird word. There's no good word about someone if you are not married. Even calling a guy you live with your boyfriend makes you sound eleven years old. Old man? If you are not living with Willie Nelson, that one doesn't work.

— *Elayne Boosler*

I have a totally wonderful new boyfriend. He calls me cutie—which is short for Chronic Urinary Tract Infection. For Valentine's Day, he gave me cranberry juice.

— *Caroline Rhea*

Boy Scout

I wanted to be a Boy Scout, but I had all the wrong traits. They were looking for kids who were trustworthy, loyal, helpful, friendly, courteous, kind, obedient, cheerful, thrifty, brave, clean, and reverent. Whereas I tended to be devious, fickle, obstructive, hostile, impolite, mean, defiant, glum, extravagant, dirty, and sacrilegious.

— *George Carlin*

Breaking Up

When I want to end relationships I just say, "I want to marry you so we can live together forever."
Sometimes they leave skid marks.

— *Rita Rudner*

I guess everyone has had that one breakup when you just want to sit in your house for six months, smoking cigarettes and eating chicken pot pies in your underwear.

— *Jake Johannsen*

Breaking up. It happens kind of suddenly. One minute you're holding hands walking down the street—and the next minute you're lying on the floor crying and all the good CDs are missing.

— *Kennedy Kasares*

When I was first asked to write an article about how women get over a broken heart I figured it would be the easiest money I ever made. Are you ready? We don't.

— *Stephanie Miller*

A lot of breakup songs have the same theme—the guy sings, "Baby, you're seeing somebody new now and if he treats you bad, I'll always be here for you 'cause I love you very much." Why don't they make that a little more realistic? "You're seeing someone new now, and if he treats you bad, good!"

— *Adam Sandler*

They say absence makes the heart grow fonder, so I figure that's why my boyfriend moved.

— *Christy Murphy*

After a breakup, I'll date anyone. If a one-legged troll who lives under a bridge glances at me twice: it's *Mardi Gras!*

— *Kris McGaha*

When it's over, it's over. And I should know. I would get into bed and she would mentally dress me.

— *Richard Lewis*

My boyfriend dumped me—or rather, I allowed him to set me free.

— *Darlene Hunt*

I broke up with my girlfriend. She moved in with another guy, and I draw the line at that.

— *Garry Shandling*

I broke up with someone, and she said, "You'll never find anyone like me again." And I'm thinking, I hope not! If I don't want you, why would I want someone just like you? Does anybody end a bad relationship and say, "By the way, do you have a twin?"

— *Larry Miller*

If your man mess up, don't leave him. To me a man is like a hell of an engine in something like a Rolls Royce. After 300,000 miles, a couple shit might happen. But don't worry. Pop the hood, fix him, he be all right. Maybe he just need an oil change.

— *Adelle Givens*

I recently broke up with this woman. Now she's bad-mouthing me. She's telling all our friends that she had to fake foreplay, that I gave her an anticlimax.

— *Richard Lewis*

The last girl I went out with blew me off. Now I call her with lame excuses to see her: "Hey, did I leave a penny over there?"

— *David Spade*

I may go back with my old boyfriend. It's really hot in my apartment, and he has air conditioning.

— *Heather McDonald*

Breasts

A lot of guys think the larger a woman's breasts are, the less intelligent she is. I think it's the opposite. I think the larger a woman's breasts are, the less intelligent the men become.

— *Anita Wise*

Japanese women inherit their breasts from their fathers.

— *Tamayo Otsuki*

I happen to like old-school seventies porn because I like the natural body. The women in this new porn, their boobs are just so weird and high and far out, they look like those goldfish with the puffy eyes.

— *Margaret Cho*

The women who got implants sued Dow Corning because they felt betrayed by their implant company. Betrayed? What, you mean I can't put a petroleum by-product in a baggie and insert it in my chest cavity, safely? I am shocked! And betrayed!

— *Dani Klein*

Breast-Feeding

It ain't easy being me—my mother breast-fed me through a straw.

— *Rodney Dangerfield*

Bus

Look at all the buses that want exact change. I figure if I give them exact change, they should take me exactly where I want to go.

— *George Wallace*

I was on a Greyhound recently. This guy was staring at my bag wondering why it closes with a zipper and not a twist tie.

— *Tom Ryan*

Bus lag: a low-level disorientation caused by riding on a bus. Almost impossible to detect.

— *George Carlin*

Cabs

I saw today a cab driver take an elderly woman across the street. No, wait a minute, the word I'm looking for is . . . knock, knock her across.

— *David Letterman*

What does it take to get a cab driver's license? I think all you need is a face. And a name with eight consonants in a row. Have you ever checked out some of the names on the license? The *O* with the line through it? What planet is that from? You need a chart of the elements just to report the guy, "Yes, Officer, his name was Amal—and then the symbol for boron."

— *Jerry Seinfeld*

I had a cab driver in Paris. The man smelled like a guy eating cheese while getting a permanent inside the septic tank of a slaughterhouse.

— *Dennis Miller*

Camping

Mexicans don't go camping in the woods, especially during hunting season. We'd be mistaken for a deer.

Somebody would go, "Your honor, I saw brown skin and brown eyes. He had his hands up. I thought they were antlers. I shot his ass."

— *Paul Rodriguez*

Cancer

You show me something that doesn't cause cancer, and I'll show you something that isn't on the market yet.

— *George Carlin*

Candy

Candy is the only reason you want to live when you're a kid. And you have your favorite candies that you love. Kids actually believe they can distinguish between twenty-one different versions of pure sugar. When I was a kid, I could taste the difference between different color M&M's. I thought the red was heartier, more of a main course M&M. And the light brown was a mellower, kind of after-dinner M.

— *Jerry Seinfeld*

The new candies get their names from things people exclaim, like Bonkers! or Nerds! And I got to thinking, geez, wouldn't it be funny if they based a line of candies on something my dad exclaims frequently? I don't know about you, but I'd get a kick out of candy called, "Where's the Damn Scotch!"

— *Bob Oshack*

Fun-size Snickers. Who's this fun for? Not me. Six or seven of those babies in a row, I'm having fun. Frustrating-size is more like it, but they can't even fit the word "frustrating" on the wrapper.

— *Jeff Garlin*

Cannibals

Cannibals love Domino's pizza. Not for the pizza, but for the delivery guy.

— *Shang*

Jeffrey Dahmer said he was temporarily insane and ate seventeen people. That ain't temporary. Somewhere around the fourth person you've got to think, "I don't think this is going away, I'm crazy."

— *Warren Hutcherson*

Capital Punishment

They showed an execution at some prison. The executioner said, "Killing a man in an electric chair is as
easy for me as going to the refrigerator and getting a
beer." I heard that and thought, "Well, scratch that
guy off my A-1 party list. He'd be partying at my
house and I'd say, "Hey, did you get my beer?" He'd
look at me funny. "Huh? I thought you said kill your
dad."

— *Bobcat Goldthwait*

Cards

They should make cards—if you're going to get a
card for somebody you don't really care about, they
should make cards that say that. "You're a friend of
my wife's cousin—the hell with you." "We hardly
know you. What did you expect, cash?"

— *Paul Reiser*

When are they gonna come up with some new
Christmas cards?

— *George Carlin*

I stayed up one night playing poker with tarot cards. I got a full house and four people died.

— *Steven Wright*

Cars

My license plate says PMS. Nobody cuts me off.

— *Wendy Liebman*

When I was a kid getting to borrow the car was a big deal. "Where are you going?" "Around the block." "How many kids are going?" "Just half a kid." Before he handed over the keys, my dad gave you a lecture. "Now I'm not giving you this car so you can screw it up." "Well," I said to myself, "then I don't want it."

— *Louie Anderson*

A New York man bought a car at a police auction, then went home and found a dead body handcuffed in the trunk. Actually it isn't that bad. This week, he can use the carpool lane.

— *Jay Leno*

My mother has this car with a computer. It talks like a Jewish car—it does, "Ehh, why even go; it's windy out."

— *Richard Lewis*

Anybody abuse rental cars? If I'm really bored I'll take one to Earl Scheib and have it painted for $29.95. This really messes up their paperwork for months and months. The thing that bothers me is when you have to return one with a full tank of gas. You know what I do now? I just top it off with a garden hose.

— *Will Shriner*

Rolls-Royce is selling its first totally new car in eighteen years. For $216,000. Sounds like a lot, but that does include the Grey Poupon. Also, the car is so luxurious that when you have an accident, instead of an airbag, a little pillow comes out with a mint on it. It's so fancy that the cupholder is a guy named Charles.

— *Jay Leno*

What's the thought process involved in purchasing a Pacer? "Got anything round and bloated, so it looks like a fish tank on wheels? With a lot of windows, so everybody knows I made a messed-up purchase?"

— *Warren Thomas*

I don't like the idea that people can call you in your car. I think there's news you shouldn't get at sixty miles per hour. "Pregnant? Whoaah!" But if we're gonna have car phones I think we should have car answering machines. "Tom's at home right now. But as soon as he goes out, he'll get back to you."

— *Tom Parks*

Cats

In my more depressed moments, I believe my cats suffer from Stockholm syndrome. You know, where the hostage falls in love with the captor, as an adaptive mechanism.

— *Betsy Salkind*

I saw a commercial for cat food that said, "All-natural food for your cat." But cat food is made out of horse meat. That's how it works in nature—the cat right above the horse on the food chain. Matter of fact, every time my kitty feels a little cooped up in his environment, I take him down to the racetrack, let him stalk some prey.

— *Norm MacDonald*

I found out why cats drink out of the toilet. My mother told me it's because it's cold in there. And I'm like, "How did my mother know that?"

— *Wendy Liebman*

My wife's cats have been neutered and declawed, so they're like pillows that eat.

— *Larry Reeb*

I gave my cat a bath the other day, they love it. He enjoyed it, it was fun for me. The fur would stick to my tongue, but other than that . . .

— *Steve Martin*

Celebrities

Bill Gates declared to the world, "I am Microsoft." Mrs. Gates had no comment.

— *Whoopi Goldberg*

I can't believe that Leonardo DiCaprio is the reason for *Titanic*'s success. Meryl Streep is a more believable leading man. It's a sad comment on our times, when women want to be be able to look at a man and think, "Yeah, I could take him in a fair fight."

— *Nosmo King*

Larry Flynt is now spokesman for organ donation. How novel of him to be hocking his own body parts for a change.

— *Betsy Salkind*

Frank Gifford quit *Monday Night Football.* Frank said it's a great job, but it's an awful lot of work and he just wanted to spend more time getting the cold shoulder from his wife and family.

— *Bill Maher*

Hugh Hefner's thirty-four-year-old wife left him for Donald Trump. When asked about it, she said that instead of being with a really old, rich guy, "I'd rather be with a really rich, old guy."

— *Conan O'Brien*

Michael Jackson is the polar opposite of President Clinton, in many respects. Michael Jackson is constantly, constantly, desperately trying to make us believe he's having sex with women.

— *David Letterman*

a b c d

Rodney King got $3.8 million and recently got his fourth DUI. He's on his way to the rare Ted Kennedy double-hat trick. He blew a .19—that's higher than my college GPA. Rodney King was drunker than I am smart. Apparently, what he meant to say was, "Can't we get a Long Island Iced Tea?"

— *Steve Marmel*

If Ted Kennedy's such a ladies' man, why does it take him nine hours to open a lady's door?

— *Dennis Miller*

I bet Kevorkian is a hard guy to hang out with. Old Jack comes over to your house and asks how are things going, you'll go, "Oh man, things are . . . good. Just get your van out of my driveway. No, I don't want to wear the happy mask tonight."

— *Jack Coen*

When John F. Kennedy Jr. and his girlfriend got married it was an uneventful ceremony. Except when the preacher asked if anyone objected to their union, half the women in America yelled out, "I do!"

— *Rosie O'Donnell*

Rush Limbaugh. Understand him for what he is—a shopping cart with a bad wheel that pulls to the right no matter which way he's facing.

— *Dennis Miller*

Madonna—everyone was so surprised when she got pregnant. I wasn't—ya drop a billion swimmers in the English Channel, one of them is going to make it to France.

— *Kris McGaha*

In *People*'s "What Did They Look Like in High School" issue, most of the celebrities were, like, twenty-one years old. They look no different. "Who would have thought that *Friends'* Jennifer Aniston was . . . a pretty girl! You'll flip when you see six-teen-year-old Jonathan Taylor Thomas as a fourteen-year-old!"

— *Tom Kenny*

At eighty-eight, the king of popcorn, Orville Redenbacher, passed away. His family is mired in an ugly dispute over whether to cremate, microwave, or air pop him.

— *Stephanie Miller*

Donald Trump doesn't have much money invested in the stock market per se. Most of his money goes into junk blondes.

— David Letterman

In an interview the Spice Girls said that their boyfriends have to take a backseat to their music. They said, "We don't let our personal lives interfere with our mediocrity."

— Conan O'Brien

Mike Tyson, former heavyweight champion, is forming a record company, Tyson Records, with lofty goals. They want to first sign the Spice Girls, then rape and eat them.

— Bill Maher

I feel I should be in charge of stopping celebrities from conspicuous consumption. When Bruce Willis bought a $250,000 house for Demi Moore's doll collection, I could have stepped in and said, "Yes, the dolls can stay, but how's about you let some human beings keep them company?"

— Jane Edith Wilson

Oprah Winfrey was cleared of charges she slandered the beef industry. It's a good thing. Can you imagine how stupid we would look to the rest of the world, if we let O.J. and Louise Woodward go free, but threw Oprah in jail for insulting a cheeseburger?

— *Jay Leno*

I'm a Native American, my father was an Oneida tribal chairman, and when I watched cowboy movies as a kid, I thought, "My dad could kick John Wayne's butt!"

— *Charlie Hill*

Child

My efforts to say nothing but positive things to my son have become desperate. "You're the best, smartest, cutest, friendliest baby, you're . . . telekinetic. You move objects with thought and start fires with your brain."

— *Andy Dick*

Since childhood is a time when kids prepare to be grown-ups, I think it makes a lot of sense to completely traumatize your children. Gets 'em ready for the real world.

— *George Carlin*

Childhood

My childhood was so bleak, I wanted to stick my head in my Easy Bake oven.

— *Mary O'Halloran*

I was kind of a negative child. As a little girl I moved all my stuff into the basement so I could be even closer to hell.

— *Penelope Lombard*

I was an only child—eventually.

— *Steven Wright*

If you're deep enough in denial to actually think that you did have a happy childhood, then your shrink will tell you that you must be forgetting something.

— *Dennis Miller*

Chunky

I'm chunky. In a bathing suit I look like a Bartlett pear with a rubber band around it.

— *Drew Carey*

Clichés

Where do clichés come from? My grandfather says,
"You just tell a couple of jokes, and you're riding the
gravy train." What is a gravy train? I didn't know
they were actually hauling gravy by rail. People
gather around big mounds of mashed potatoes waiting for the 5:15 gravy to show up?

— *Rich Hall*

Cloning

Dolly the cloned sheep got pregnant in the old-
fashioned, conventional way—by a shepherd.

— *Bill Maher*

Cloning is expensive and scary. This could mean that
Ross Perot could run in every presidential election for
the next 2,000 years.

— *Argus Hamilton*

"Human cloning would not lead to identical souls,
because only God can create a soul," a panel set up
by Pope John Paul has concluded. They also took

care of a couple other things that were burning issues: apparently, Trix are indeed for kids.

— *Janeane Garofalo*

Codependent

I was so mean to my old boyfriend he went to Codependents Anonymous, and I used to page him there.

— *Mary O'Halloran*

I'm not codependent myself, but aren't they great to have around?

— *Betsy Salkind*

Coffee

They just opened a new Starbucks, in my living room.

— *Janeane Garofalo*

Every time I buy a cup of coffee in a coffee house there's a box to send money to the kids in Colombia. Colombia should be a superpower by now. They produce coffee and cocaine. It's not like they can't figure out how to motivate the workers.

— *Margot Black*

Is it possible to get a cup of coffee-flavored coffee anymore in this country? What happened with coffee? Did I miss a meeting? They have every other flavor but coffee-flavored coffee. They have mochaccino, frappaccino, cappuccino, al pacino. Coffee doesn't need a menu, it needs a cup.

— *Denis Leary*

College

I was thrown out of NYU. On my metaphysics final I looked within the soul of the boy sitting next to me.

— *Woody Allen*

I had the worst study habits in the history of college, until I found out what I was doing wrong—highlighting with black magic marker.

— *Jeff Altman*

I took biology two years in a row just to eat the specimens.

— *Pat Paulsen*

I went to college—majored in Philosophy. My father said, "Why don't you minor in Communications so you can wonder out loud?"

— *Mike Dugan*

I went to the University of South Florida for five and a half years. Then I sobered up, got dressed, and went home—they still have my earrings.

— *Tracy Smith*

When it came to joining a fraternity, I rolled a seven. The friends that I made have been lifelong, and the lessons I learned were invaluable. I'll admit that I haven't had a chance to use what I learned about parliamentary procedure, and I've never again had to make a bong out of a toilet paper roll, but who knows? Someday I might.

— *Drew Carey*

I was so stoned in college that when my mom would call I would still keep smoking out of my bong. She'd hear the bubbles and say, "What's going on over there—are you sinking?"

— *Scott Silverman*

You learn how to wash clothes different in college. At home you have "colors," "delicate" . . . in college, "dirty," "DIRTY!" and "*funky*."

— *Sinbad*

Comedy

Comedy is the ability to make people laugh without making them puke.

— *Steve Martin*

Stand-up comedy hasn't changed. It's still the last refuge of the bitter alcoholic.

— *Bob Odenkirk*

Communication

I have e-mail, a pager, a cell phone, a fax line. I've got an answering machine, three phone lines at home, one in my purse, and a phone in my car. The only excuse I have if I don't return your call is I just don't like you.

— *Alicia Brandt*

That movie *Fatal Attraction* really ruined things for women. I mean, you can't even call a guy a hundred and fifty times a day anymore without having them get all bent out of shape.

— *Lisa Goich*

If I had a vibrating pager, I would get a mobile phone and call myself. Stand around hitting redial all day.

— *Dan Wilson*

The best device we have in our house is the baby intercom, a kind of walkie-talkie that lets you monitor your kid from other rooms. So my daughter's in the crib with one part of the intercom, and I'm in the other. Then all of a sudden, I hear her crackling over the static, "Breaker, one-nine, Daddy. I've got spit-up on my shirt and I'm packing a load. Please, come help me out."

— *Bob Saget*

I read that 28 percent of Americans think they can communicate with the dead. The other 72 percent switched back to AT&T.

— *Bobcat Zany*

Computers

The term "surfing the Net" is an insult to surfers—and nets. I was on this web site called "I Just Got Out of the Shower." It's people from around the world talking about how they're still a little wet. And when you get dry, you get off it. Isn't it great how the Internet is going to bring us all together?

— *Bob Odenkirk*

I'm very behind when it comes to technology. My friends all want me to get a computer. I just got a cotton gin, and I can't figure out how to work that. I'm on the phone every day with tech support, "Do I keep the seeds, or the fuzzy stuff?"

— *Matt Weinhold*

I don't own a computer. I'm waiting for the kind where I can look at the screen and say, "Hey, I need a pizza," and one comes out and hits me in the eyebrows.

— *Kathleen Madigan*

When I'm around hard-core computer geeks I wanna say, "Come outside, the graphics are great!"

— *Matt Weinhold*

Condoms

My sister is a Disney freak; for Christmas she gave me their condoms. My favorite was the Mickey one, ya know, 'cuz of the ears. And for the Pinocchio ones all I had to do was get my boyfriend to lie, which wasn't hard.

— *Penny Wiggins*

Even though I'm single again, I'm still buying condoms. I don't want the woman at the store to think that I've stopped having sex. I don't really think that's any of her business. Although the condoms are piling up, so I'm going to have to have a lucky streak or think of a crafts project.

— *Jake Johannsen*

There's this one ad on TV, but it's the wrong approach. A woman says, "It's not worth dying for." Well, that's not going to work. Because when you are in the act, it kind of is worth dying for. If they want to sell condoms, they should be more positive. The ads should say, "Look, buy condoms and you'll stay up for years."

— *Elayne Boosler*

Recently someone asked if I minded wearing a condom. Au contraire, I prefer them. There's no difference in the sensation, unless you count the total lack of any.

— *Richard Jeni*

I'm not embarrassed to buy condoms. It's not like when you first buy them and you mix them in with a bunch of other stuff as if you don't know that you're getting them. I don't get that theory. "Oh, condoms? I didn't know they were in there. But thanks guy, put them in the bag. I'll find some damn use for them." Hopefully, I'll have the same attitude later when I have to buy really embarrassing stuff, like adult diapers.

— *Jake Johannsen*

I was insecure about sex. I've grown more secure. I used to use the amateur phylactics, and I only use the prophylactics now.

— *Steve Martin*

Magnum condoms are a marketing gimmick, because what guy is going to admit he doesn't require them? "No thanks, they're so big on me, I need to use a twist tie."

— *Robert Schimmel*

Read the condom boxes, they're pretty funny. Trojans say, "New shape." I didn't know this was necessary. Must have been that Chernobyl incident. Another box said, "Reservoir," I said. "You mean these things can actually generate hydroelectric power?"

— *Elayne Boosler*

Nobody's passing out condoms to increase the sexual activity of kids. Condoms don't make babies—people do.

— *Dennis Miller*

Cooking

My husband says I feed him like he's a god; every meal is a burnt offering.

— *Rhonda Hansome*

Every time I go near the stove, the dog howls.

— *Phyllis Diller*

There's a big boom in Irish culture right now. I was in Barnes and Noble the other day and I saw a book entitled Irish cuisine and I laughed my balls off. What are we famous for cuisine-wise? We put everything in a pot and we boil it for seventeen and a half hours straight, until you can eat it with a straw. That's not cuisine, that's penance.

— *Denis Leary*

Cosmetics

I can't stand makeup commercials. "Do you need a lipstick that keeps your lips kissable?" No, I need a lipstick that gets me equal pay for equal work. How about eye shadow that makes me stop thinking I'm too fat?

— *Heidi Joyce*

Take it from me, wrinkle cream doesn't work. I've been using it for two years and my balls still look like raisins.

— *Harland Williams*

Crime

I was walking through the park. I had a very bad asthmatic attack. These three asthmatics attacked me. I know . . . I should have heard them hiding.

— *Emo Philips*

I don't buy temporary insanity as a murder defense. 'Cause people kill people, that's an animal instinct. I think breaking into someone's home and redecorating it is temporary insanity.

— *Sue Kolinsky*

I was arrested today for scalping low numbers at the deli.

— *Richard Lewis*

I have six locks on my door, all in a row, and when I go out I only lock every other lock. 'Cause I figure no matter how long somebody stands there, picks the locks, they're always locking three.

— *Elayne Boosler*

I used to eat while I was in the supermarket. I guess I didn't consider it stealing 'cause I took it out inside my body.

— *Arsenio Hall*

"Crime of passion"—that phrase drives me crazy. A man murdering his girlfriend is not a crime of passion. Premature ejaculation—that's a crime of passion.

— *Hellura Lyle*

Sex offenders in the state of Delaware now have to put that on their driver's license. So that every time you cash a check or whatever, it says "sex offender." It's kind of like that sticker that says, "organ donor," but this is a very specific organ donated.

— *Bill Maher*

My friend Larry's in jail now. He got twenty-five years for something he didn't do. He didn't run fast enough.

— *Damon Wayans*

Remember that 560-pound criminal who was released from jail because he had asthma? He claimed jail was bad for him. Who made up this rule? I thought jail was supposed to be a little bit bad for you. Apparently not anymore. Apparently now it's like, "Sorry, claustrophobia. Can't go. Wish I could. Sorry." The electric chair? "No way. Even a heating pad gives me a rash."

— *Paula Poundstone*

All black men are born suspects. When I came out of my mother, if anything happened within a three-block radius, I was a suspect. The day I was born somebody's car got stolen from the hospital parking lot. They made me stand in a lineup. That was pretty tough considering I wasn't even a day old and couldn't crawl, much less walk. Good thing I had a couple black nurses to hold me up. I got lucky. They were in the lineup, too.

— *Chris Rock*

Cuddling

When did cuddling go out of style, when did that become a bad thing? Last night I was making love— with a prostitute—and she gets up to walk out the door—the car door—and I'm like, "What about my needs, Miss?"

— *David Cross*

Cults

Heaven's Gate cult members were all huge *Star Trek* heads. Surprise, Trekkies are kooks! There's never been a mass suicide by the fans of *Green Acres* or *That Girl.*

— *Tom Kenny*

Cults just aren't any fun anymore. How did we get from crazy longhaired guys yelling, "Let's take acid and fuck!" to a bunch of people with matching hair- cuts killing themselves on bunk beds? In the sixties they also believed they'd be riding on a flying saucer, but they knew they'd be coming down in a few hours.

— *Mike Maron*

Dance

The Lord of the Dance: You want to do that show the right way? Get some big, fat, beer-bellied Irish guys, and let them dance and drink and punch their relatives at the same time.

— *Denis Leary*

Dating

It's too much trouble to get laid. 'Cause you have to go out with a guy, and go to dinner with him, and listen to him talk about his opinions. And I don't have that kind of time.

— *Kathy Griffin*

I hate dating. You look for just the right girl. Right figure, right face. You search until you find her and then, for no apparent reason, your binoculars fog up.

— *Mike Bullard*

They say there is a right person born for everybody. I just get scared that my guy might have died at birth.

— *Brenda Pontiff*

I deserve someone who likes me for who I am . . . pretending to be.

— *Arj Barker*

Dating is dumb. Basically you're making false judgments based on false exteriors. Oh, sure, my superficial self likes your superficial self, but the real me likes your roommate.

— *Margot Black*

I'd just like to meet a girl with a head on her shoulders—I hate necks.

— *Steve Martin*

Whenever I want a really nice meal, I start dating again.

— *Susan Healy*

I was out on a date recently and the guy took me horseback riding. That was kind of fun, until we ran out of quarters.

— *Susie Loucks*

Dating in your twenties is like getting a science project. "What did you get? I got an alcoholic; I'm going to change him!"

— *Caroline Rhea*

I tell men, if you want to impress a woman don't send her flowers, send her a maid. Because if you spend $55 on a dozen roses, they're dead the next day. A maid costs about $40 and you still have $15 dollars left to get Chinese food and one rose. By the time you come over we haven't cleaned, and you have food, a rose, and you. Baby, we'll do you all night long.

— *Luda Vika*

I asked this one girl out and she said, "You got a friend?" I said yes, she said, "Then go out with him."

— *Dom Irrera*

I've been on so many blind dates I should get a free dog.

— *Wendy Liebman*

My grandmother wanted me to go to church to meet women. My grandmother wanted me to work the church—that's wrong, ain't it? "Praise the lord! Hey, how ya doing? Nice dress. Look I'm going to go over there get some of this wine and crackers, want some?"

— *Warren Hutcherson*

Here are three things I never want to hear again on a first date, "So. . . how much cash do you have on you?" "Wow! You're a big girl! How much do you weigh?" "Wanna hold my gun? It's loaded." Too bad that one wasn't a metaphor, 'cuz then I would have.

— *Jennifer Fairbanks*

I met a new girl at a barbecue. A very pretty blond girl, I think. I don't know for sure. Her hair was on fire. And all she talked about was herself. "I'm on fire!" You know the type. "Jesus Christ, help me! Put me out!" Come on, can we talk about me a little bit?

— *Garry Shandling*

What is a date really, but a job interview that lasts all night? The only difference is that in not many job interviews is there a chance you'll wind up naked.

— *Jerry Seinfeld*

I once dated a guy who drank coffee and alcohol at the same time. What a prince. Bad breath, limp dick, and wouldn't go to sleep.

— *Kris McGaha*

My favorite kind of guys to go out with are guys from another country. I like foreign guys 'cause you can tell them anything. "Ahmed, it's customary in America that you pay my rent on the first date."

— *Ellen Cleghorne*

I was a horrible date all through school and college. Here's an impression of me on a date in high school: "Come on, chug it!"

— *David Spade*

I went out with this one guy, I was very excited about it. He took me out to dinner, he made me laugh—he made me pay. He's like, "Oh, I'm sorry. I forgot my wallet." "Really? I forgot my vagina."

— *Lisa Sunstedt*

I hate singles' bars. Guys come up to me and say, "Hey, cupcake, can I buy you a drink?" I say, "No, but I'll take the three bucks."

— *Margaret Smith*

I'd like to be a fish fly. It's a bug that only lives one day. That's right, they're born, they mate, they die. Kinda takes all the worry out of, "Will he ever call me again?"

— *Lisa Goich*

When you're first single, you're so optimistic. At the beginning, you're like, "I want to meet a guy who's really smart, really sweet, really good-looking, has a really great career." Six months later, you're like, "Lord, any mammal with a day job."

— *Carol Leifer*

People are going on dates now to coffee bars. This is the worst idea. Four cappuccinos later, your date doesn't look any better.

— *Margot Black*

She wanted a signing bonus when we went steady.

— *Richard Lewis*

To me, guys in bars are all the same, white collar, blue collar, flea collar. They all just sniff around, scratch, and then look for a place to bury their bone.

— *Pamela Yager*

I don't need to be rich, I'd just like to have enough money that I can take a woman out to dinner once, without worrying if my father's credit card bill is paid up. Actually, I'd just like to take a woman out to dinner once. The last time I had a date, Prince had a name and Kurt Cobain had a face.

— *Peter Berkowitz*

Have you ever dated someone because you were too lazy to commit suicide?

— *Judy Tenuta*

I'm still going on bad dates, when by now I should be in a bad marriage.

— *Laura Kightlinger*

I was dating this girl for two years—and right away the nagging starts: "I wanna know your name."

— *Mike Binder*

My sister was with two men in one night. She could hardly walk after that. Can you imagine? Two dinners!

— *Sarah Silverman*

I have one pick-up line that never works. If I'm at a club and I see a guy I like I smile and if he smiles back and I feel really comfortable I'll walk over and say, "Stick it in!"

— *Margaret Cho*

Literally everyone I know is having a baby and I'm childless—except for this boy that I'm dating. He's so young he has that new car smell. Yummy. Fresh wax.

— *Caroline Rhea*

Men date thin girls because they're too weak to argue and salads are cheap.

— *Jennifer Fairbanks*

Sometimes I'd rather stay home and watch the new HBO movie of the week than go out to a bar and see reruns of guys I've dated.

— *Pamela Yager*

The older you get the lower your standards get. I used to be so picky. Oh, when I get married he's going to be tall, handsome, rich . . . and I'm down to: registered voter. I'd marry a midget just for the handicapped parking.

— *Kathleen Madigan*

I'm dating a guy who's twenty-one. That's seven in boy years.

— *Lisa Goich*

I dated a younger man, but we had nothing in common. I asked him where he was when Elvis died. He was in amniotic fluid.

— *Robin Roberts*

The last guy I dated bought his condoms at Baby Gap.

— *Suzanne Flagge*

Daughter

Three daughters and people ask, "Were you upset that the third child was a girl?" I say, "No, not at all. I'm whittling a boy out of wood right now."

— *Bob Saget*

Dead End

I'm living on a one-way, dead-end street. I don't know how I got there.

— *Steven Wright*

Death

I don't mind death—I just don't want to be there when it happens.

— *Woody Allen*

If Shaw and Einstein couldn't beat death, what chance have I got? Practically none.

— *Mel Brooks*

Immortality is a long shot, I admit. But somebody has to be first.

— *Bill Cosby*

Death is the last big move of your life. The hearse is like the van, the pallbearers are your close friends, the only ones you could really ask to help you with a big move like that. And the casket is that great, perfect box you've been looking for your whole life. The only problem is once you find it, you're in it.

— *Jerry Seinfeld*

My grandmother was upset at my grandfather's funeral: "You've got him in a brown suit, I wanted him in a blue suit." The mortician said, "That's okay, ma'am, we'll take care of it right now. Ed, switch the heads on two and four."

— *Bill Bauer*

My uncle was a clown for the Ringling Brothers Circus, and when he died all of his friends went to the funeral in one car.

— *Steven Wright*

I got a coupon in the mail: Ash Burial at Sea, $478. What an affordable way to die. The only thing is, I don't want my ashes scattered at sea. I want them thrown on all the people who have ever blown smoke in my face. Let's see if their dry cleaners can get that out.

— *Cathy Ladman*

Texas killed another one. It was kind of a grisly death on death row, because the guy did not go easy. The first attempt failed and they just kind of wounded him. It was tough for observers to watch, and it was also very embarrassing for the executioner, 'cause this was "Take your daughter to work day."

— *Bill Maher*

I was thinking about committing suicide but I have a tendency to procrastinate, so I just kept putting it off. They say procrastination is a bad thing, but it saved my life.

— *Shashi Bhatia*

I believe Dr. Kevorkian is onto something. I think he's great. Because suicide is our way of saying to God, "You can't fire me. I quit."

— *Bill Maher*

I can't believe that book *Final Exit* was on the best-seller list. I saw a guy buying it who was depressed because it cost seventeen bucks. I told him, "Sir, I'll stab you in the head for four." But he bought the book and paid for it in cash. And I'm going, "If you're going to kill yourself, why not charge it?"

— *Kathleen Madigan*

Anybody can commit suicide, but nobody ever does anything cool with it. If I ever commit suicide I'm going to fling myself off the top of a skyscraper, but before I do I'm going to fill my pockets with candy and gum. That way when the onlookers walk up they can go, "Oh—Snickers, hey!"

— *Patton Oswalt*

Debt

Strange things happen when you're in debt. Two weeks ago, my car broke down and my phone got disconnected. I was one electric bill away from being Amish.

— *Tom Ryan*

Democrats vs. Republicans

A Democrat sees the glass of water as half-full. A Republican looks at the same glass, and wonders who the hell drank half his glass of water.

— *Jeff Cesario*

Diet

If you eat enough celery sticks and Dexedrine, somebody's gonna get killed. Either you'll keel over while trying to walk up a flight of stairs, or you'll end up shooting someone just to watch them die.

— *Drew Carey*

Do you have to brush your teeth during a fast? Why do they call it a fast if it goes so damn slow?

— *Gallagher*

You know you're on a diet when cat food commercials make you hungry.

— *Andy Bumatai*

I'm trying to get back to my original weight—eight pounds, three ounces.

— *Cheril Vendetti*

I went on that new fourteen-day diet, and all I lost was two weeks.

— *Sheila Kay*

I want to lose ten pounds. I just don't know if I should start power walking or smoking.

— *Lisa Goich*

I was on the grapefruit diet. For breakfast I ate fifteen grapefruit. Now when I go to the bathroom I keep squirting myself in the eye.

— *Max Alexander*

When I was in college I got out of control dieting. There were two food groups for me: prepackaged diet foods and alcoholic beverages. I was a bulimic-anorexic wannabe, but my drinking always held me back.

— *Merrill Markoe*

There's a new diet that's guaranteed to make you as thin as the supermodels. The first two days, you can eat anything you want. The third day, you're taken hostage in Lebanon for seven years.

— *Heidi Joyce*

They say that exercise and proper diet are the keys to a longer, healthier life. Watch for my next book, *How I Died While Jogging*.

— *Drew Carey*

I have a great diet. You're allowed to eat anything you want, but you must eat it with naked fat people.

— *Ed Bluestone*

Dining

Waiters and waitresses are becoming much nicer and more caring. I used to pay my check, they'd say, "Thank you." That graduated into "Have a nice day." That's now escalated into "You take care of yourself, now." The other day I paid my check—the waiter said, "Don't put off that mammogram."

— *Rita Rudner*

The only comfort you can take from eating at a Denny's is that you know for sure that all over America, everyone else at a Denny's is just as unhappy as you are.

— *Drew Carey*

You never go to Denny's, you end up there. Their slogan should be, "Hey, it's late." Some lady was complaining about her food there. That's like complaining you went to a whorehouse and didn't get loved.

— *Warren Thomas*

The other night I ate at a real nice family restaurant. Every table had an argument going.

— *George Carlin*

I stopped for breakfast at the International House of Pancakes. As soon as you walk in the establishment, you catch the distinct, worldwide feel of the place. I was completely baffled by the complex menu. So I just had the *flapjack du jour* and my syrup steward helped me select a very dry maple that was busy but never precocious.

— *Dennis Miller*

Discrimination

Mexicans don't even get into Taco Bell commercials—you'd think we'd at least have a shot at that shit. And their slogan was "Run for the Border." Hey, white people, that's racist. How would you like, "Denny's has good crackers—for the cracker in you."

— *Carlos Mencia*

Divorce

It is a sad fact that 50 percent of marriages in this country end in divorce. But hey, the other half end in death. You could be one of the lucky ones!

— *Richard Jeni*

My wife and I had an amicable divorce. She lets me see my stuff on weekends. Last Sunday I took my sweaters to Disneyland.

— *Craig Shoemaker*

When I divorced I went through the various stages of grieving—anger, denial—and dancing around with my settlement check.

— *Maura Kennedy*

Our parents got divorced when we were kids and it was kind of cool. We got to go to divorce court with them. It was like a game show. My mom won the house and car. We were all excited. My dad got some luggage.

— *Tom Arnold*

I love Ireland, but they're a tad behind the times—they just voted divorce in last year. We're two years away from the millennium, we're about to colonize Mars, and they just voted divorce in. Wow, hang on for another 2,000 years and you might get the Playboy channel.

— *Denis Leary*

Doctors

Interns scare me. They're too young. How can you have confidence in a doctor who has his rubber gloves pinned to his sleeves?

— *Joan Rivers*

I recently went to a new doctor and noticed he was located in something called the Professional Building. I felt better right away.

— *George Carlin*

I've got a doctor's appointment on Monday. I'm not sick or anything. It's just that I lost some weight, and I want someone to see me naked.

— *Tracy Smith*

I understand that the doctor had to spank me when I was born, but I really don't see any reason he had to call me a whore.

— *Sarah Silverman*

I've been feeling kind of lousy for the past few weeks. I don't want to go to the doctor because I just know what he's gonna say: "Stop shooting heroin." What a broken record that guy is.

— *Drake Sather*

Doctors are crooks. Why do you think they wear gloves? Not for sanitary reasons—fingerprints.

— *Jackie Mason*

Be suspicious of any doctor who tries to take your temperature with his finger.

— *David Letterman*

How come every time you go to the emergency room they got doctors from India there? I don't want to put my life in the hands of any doctor who believes in reincarnation. Give me a good old-fashioned American doctor who'll make sure you live to pay that bill.

— *Glen Super*

Dogs

A Canadian psychologist is selling a video that teaches you how to test your dog's IQ. Here's how it works: If you spend $12.99 for the video, your dog is smarter than you.

— *Jay Leno*

My friend George walked his dog, all at once. Walked him from Boston to Ft. Lauderdale, and said, "Now you're done."

— *Steven Wright*

Oh, that dog! All he does is piddle. He's nothing but a fur-covered kidney that barks.

— *Phyllis Diller*

Dogs lead a nice life. You never see a dog with a wristwatch.

— *George Carlin*

Doberman pinschers catch them some bad mother-fuckers, they fast. They catch the average white boy. By the time they catch a nigger, though, they too tired to do anything.

— *Richard Pryor*

Milk Bone dog biscuit commercials showed dogs being ashamed of their bad breath. Those were realistic. I think if my dog was concerned about his breath, he'd stop eating his own vomit.

— *Drake Sather*

Clinton's pet Labrador, Buddy, is getting neutered. The dog will never have sex again. Overnight, they've turned Buddy from a Democrat into a Republican.

— *Jay Leno*

I have a Dachshund. It curses when it barks. Why? You would too if you were dragging your balls on the sidewalk.

— *Billy Connolly*

I have a dog that's half pit bull, half poodle. Not much of a guard dog, but a vicious gossip.

— *Craig Shoemaker*

I just bought a Chihuahua. It's the dog for lazy people. You don't have to walk it. Just hold it out the window and squeeze.

— *Anthony Clark*

They have dog food for constipated dogs. If your dog is constipated, why screw up a good thing? Stay indoors and let 'em bloat.

— *David Letterman*

I bought a dog for $500 and my friend says, "Give me $500 and I'll shit on your carpet."

— *Ellen Cleghorne*

I like driving around with my two dogs, especially on the freeways. I make them wear little hats so I can use the car pool lanes.

— *Monica Piper*

Dream

This morning I woke up out of a dream, and I went right into a daydream.

— *Steven Wright*

Driving

When I'm driving here I see a sign that says, CAU-
TION: SMALL CHILDREN PLAYING. I slow down, and
then it occurs to me: I'm not afraid of small children.

— *Jonathan Katz*

One time we were driving through a construction
zone and the sign said, SPEED LIMIT 35 AHEAD. And
there were four of us. We were through there in no
time.

— *Geechy Guy*

My mom's the worst driver. She drives in that imagi-
nary lane. "What are you doing over here, Mom?"
"No one's in it."

— *Louie Anderson*

The highway cop said, "Walk a straight line." I said,
"Well, Officer Pythagoras, the closest you could ever
come to achieving a straight line would be making an
electroencephalogram of your own brain waves." He
said, "You're under arrest. You have the right to
remain silent. Do you wish to retain that right?" I
thought, "Oooh, a paradox!"

— *Emo Philips*

I was stopped once for going fifty-three in a thirty-five-mile zone, but I told 'em I had dyslexia.

— *Spanky*

The gas station attendant looks at the car and says, "You got a flat tire." I said, "No, the other three just swelled up."

— *Bill Engvall*

I hate driving, and I hate when people honk at me. Unless I'm making a left turn. Then I like it because that's how I know it's time to turn.

— *Rita Rudner*

I think all cars should have car phones in 'em and their license plates should be their phone number. So you can call 'em up and tell 'em to get the hell out of the way. Old people would have 800 numbers.

— *John Mendoza*

Driving hasn't been the same since I installed fun-house rearview mirrors.

— *Steven Wright*

My mom taught me how to drive. I can't drive worth a damn, but I can change all my clothes at a stoplight.

— *Craig Shoemaker*

Drugs

It's not called cocaine anymore. It's now referred to as "Crack Classic."

— *Billiam Coronel*

When my PTA was looking for fund-raising ideas I suggested, "Hey, let's sell crack! Not to our kids—but there's a public school down the street."

— *Bobcat Goldthwait*

I took acid one night and had an argument with a Paul Westerberg CD.

— *Greg Behrendt*

I've asked, "What is it about cocaine that makes it so wonderful?" And they say, "Well, it intensifies your personality." Yes, but what if you're an asshole?

— *Bill Cosby*

You always get drugs when you go and see the doctor with the baby. The drugs are for me and Mama.

— *Gallagher*

I'm not pro-drug. They obviously cause a lot of damage. But I am pro-logic, and you're never going to stop the human need for release through altered consciousness. The government could take away all the drugs in the world and people would spin around on their lawn until they fell down and saw God.

— *Dennis Miller*

There are obvious times when you don't want people getting high. I wouldn't want my surgeon to get high before my operation. If I'm laying there on the gurney, the last thing I want to hear is, "Nurse, gimme one of those, um, pointy things. Now, refresh my memory—we're doing what here? No shit!"

— *David Cross*

Drugs don't enhance your creativity. You get the same old results with heroin. Your neighbors will complain when the ambulance shows up like clockwork. The firemen are going to track footprints on the rug. Your baby's going to keep waking up because of the guy shouting, "1, 2, 3—clear!" And you always lose your job. Your boss says, "It happened on Monday and twice on Tuesday—you died. We can't have that here, there are plenty of other bike messengers."

— *Paul Alexander*

You should always say no to drugs. That will drive the prices down.

— *Geechy Guy*

My drug of choice is the antidepressant Zoloft. I think of it as an airbag for my mind. As soon as things start getting too rowdy . . . *Poof!* . . . Aaahh . . .

— *Dana Gould*

A detox center is where you pay $15,000 to find out that twelve-step meetings are free.

— **Mark Lundholm**

In this Holiday Inn in Florida, I noticed a sign on the wall: THIS IS A DRUG-FREE WORKPLACE. I thought, Why are they giving us this information? Two years ago did they have a sign that said, THE BELL STAFF IS AS HIGH AS A KITE? It seemed odd to have the virtues of the staff right up there on the wall. MANY OF OUR STAFF READ.

— *Paula Poundstone*

Pot is just God's way of saying, "Hi." I mean, what's wrong with a drug that lets you appreciate Joni Mitchell just that much more?

— *Taylor Negron*

I'm one of those people who can't operate a screwdriver, but I could roll a joint in a twister.

— **Scott Thompson**

In high school, my brother Bill would occasionally sell pot out of the family basement without our parents' knowledge. And my mother was always saying things like, "Oh, that Bill is so popular! But why do his friends only stay for five minutes?"

— *Julia Sweeney*

I recently attended a pro-drug rally—in my basement.

— *David Cross*

I've been trying to quit smoking pot. It was easier to become a vegetarian, because your friends will never show up at your house with a sack of beef saying, "*Star Trek's* on—twist up a link!"

— *Brian Posehn*

If you're new to antidepressants, try the new Flintstones Prozac formulated for anyone who's sad and has three toes.

— *Leslie Nesbitt*

The war on drugs is a big waste of money. The government is pissing it away just so they can put on a big show for the people who are against drugs—just because those people happen to vote. See, I don't think marijuana smokers get to the voting booth as often as they'd like to. "What, it was yesterday?"

— *Drew Carey*

Why is there such controversy about drug testing? I know plenty of guys who'd be willing to test any drug they can come up with.

— *George Carlin*

I'll tell you when I stopped doing Quaaludes—when they stopped making them.

— *Judy Toll*

New information indicates that the planes that brought weapons to the Contras returned to the United States filled with cocaine. Which means that, while Nancy Reagan was saying, "Just say no," the CIA was saying, "Just fly low."

— *Paul Krassner*

Dry Cleaners

I put my clothes in the cleaners and then don't have the money to get them out. It's like they're in jail waiting on me to spring 'em.

— *Paula Poundstone*

efg

Earthquakes

One way to tell when you're having an earthquake is—your Jell-O stands still.

— *Soupy Sales*

People in California just don't care about earth-quakes. They are apathetic. "Oh, look, the ground's opening up. Oh, there goes my house. There goes my wife and kids. My car! Oh, crap, my Beamer! How am I going to get to work? Oh, there goes work! All right! *Party!*" I'm just scared there's going to be a major earthquake at the time I'm getting a vasectomy.

— *Bob Saget*

Eating Disorders

I went to a conference for bulimics and anorexics. It was a nightmare—the bulimics ate the anorexics. But it was okay, because they were back again in ten minutes.

— *Monica Piper*

Ecology

Remember—a developer is someone who wants to build a house in the woods. An environmentalist is someone who already owns a house in the woods.

— *Dennis Miller*

I had a great Earth Day. I drove around with my muffler off, flicking butts out the window, then I hit a deer.

— *Drew Carey*

Underground nuclear testing, defoliation of the rain forests, toxic waste—let's put it this way, if the world were a big apartment, we wouldn't get our deposit back.

— *John Ross*

Do you ever wonder where all the farts go? They go up into the atmosphere and they form the fart zone. It's right above the ozone layer, and that's why we have to protect the ozone layer!

— *Steve Martin*

I'm glad there's a big old hole in the ozone—'cause you can get a tan in a split second. "Hey, I'm starting to bubble up like a bad paint job. I'm saving money on X rays—I can see where I broke my arm as a kid."

— *Joe Keyes*

The other day I bought a wastepaper basket and carried it home in a paper bag. And when I got home I put the paper bag in the basket,

— *Lily Tomlin*

Economics

I am heavily in debt. Right now my goal in life is to be just broke. I wanna get back to zero. Someday, I'm gonna have nothing. I'll leave it to my kids. "See this? None of this is all yours."

— *Tom Ryan*

No matter how much money you make, you always need an extra $40 a week. I'm sure it was Einstein who first stated: "Expense equals salary plus forty bucks."

— *Jeffrey Jena*

A study of economics usually reveals that the best time to buy anything is last year.

— *Marty Allen*

The economy is incredibly good. It's too good. It's happy, it's excited. The GNP is up, the Dow Jones is up. Inflation is at its lowest level since 1963. I went to the ATM today, and I inserted my card—it moaned.

— *Bill Maher*

We survived the 1980s. Back then, the economic program was called "trickle down." That actually meant they were pissing on you. How the whole theory goes was this: "We have all the money. If we drop some, it's yours. Go for it."

— *Bill Maher*

Education

I majored in animal husbandry in college, which is good, 'cause I married a couple of pigs.

— *Sheila Kay*

Ejaculation, Premature

Premature ejaculation, I don't believe in that. If I come, it was right on time, that's the way I see it. As far as I'm concerned I can't come fast enough. They're mad at me because we have different goals in sex: I'm a speedfucker.

— *Dave Chapelle*

It happens to everybody. When it happens to me, I say, "Hey, you know, it's just my way of saying that I'm happy to see you."

— *Richard Lewis*

My psychologist told me that a lot of men suffer from premature ejaculation. That's not true—women suffer.

— *Robert Schimmel*

Employment

I was a ballerina. I had to quit after I injured a groin muscle. It wasn't mine.

— *Rita Rudner*

This is going to sound odd, but it's absolutely true. Dr. Kevorkian has hired an apprentice, so he'll be able to assist in more suicides. Apparently Kevorkian pays well, but he has the country's worst health plan.

— *Conan O'Brien*

I majored in nursing. I had to drop it. I ran out of milk.

— *Judy Tenuta*

I used to work at the International House of Pancakes. I know what you are thinking. Why? How's that possible? But you set your goals and go for them. I made it happen. It was the worst job I ever had in my entire life. When people were rude to me, I touched their eggs. It's true. I flipped them over in the back with my hand. Four times. They didn't know, but I felt better.

— *Paula Poundstone*

The phrase Minimum Wage—What does that do for your self-esteem? Can't we think of something else we can call it? Well, It's Better Than Nothing Wage, I'm making the At Least I Don't Live in Haiti Wage.

— *David Cross*

I have a friend who's collecting unemployment insurance. This guy has never worked so hard in his life as he has to keep this thing going. He's down there every week, waiting on the lines and getting interviewed and making up all these lies about looking for jobs. If they had any idea of the effort and energy that he is expending to avoid work, I'm sure they'd give him a raise.

— *Jerry Seinfeld*

You can't believe how much hard work it is to con people into thinking that you're productive and busy. Always thinking up things to tell them you're going to do tomorrow, having to exaggerate every minute of your nowhere day . . . it's worse than having a job. At least when you're employed, when people ask about your day you can tell them to shut up and mind their own business.

— *Drew Carey*

People make a living donating to sperm banks. Last year I let $500 slip through my fingers.

— *Robert Schimmel*

Engagement

That night is the most romantic we guys get. I remember when I asked my wife to marry me, I got down on my knee and I was shaking a little stick and

I went, "Ooops, that's not the color we're looking for, is it, honey?" I get teary-eyed just thinking about it.

— *Jack Coen*

I fell in love and I thought she fell in love with me, too. Are you familiar with the situation? I sat with an engagement ring, waiting for a response. I was a single guy with an engagement ring. It was like having a loaded gun laying around the house. I was frightened I'd marry somebody by accident.

— *Jake Johannsen*

Entertainment

I wasn't being entertained for over twenty minutes yesterday, and I started suffering withdrawal. I didn't have a TV on, no book to read, no music playing, no video games, nothing. I got scared and sweaty and began shaking and wondered: Would I ever be entertained again? I was just about to feel an emotion— yes, an emotion inspired by real life—I mean it was just around the bend, and in the nick of time I made it to a cereal box and read the ingredients. Thank you, God!

— *Bob Odenkirk*

Ethics

What's right is what's left if you do everything wrong.

— Robin Williams

Ethnic

Black folks have the coolest names—Arsenio, Oprah. And when my wife was thinking up names for the baby, I said why can't we be black and just make up a name? That's what black people do. You guys could be making love in the backseat of the Toyota, and name the kid Tercel.

— Bobcatby Slayton

White friends, black people do not all look alike. It is you that look alike. All of you all are just white. Look at us, pecan, yellow, bright, black, mahogany.

— Redd Foxx

Black namcs sound more like products you'd find in the drugstore. "My name is Advil, this is my wife, Cloret. Tylenol, you wanna turn the TV down, it's givin' me a headache! And the twins, Murine and Visine . . ."

— *Daryl Sivad*

My husband is English and I'm American. I wonder what our children would be like. They'd probably be rude, but disgusted by their own behavior.

— *Rita Rudner*

I'm Irish Catholic, and drinking is such a pervasive part of life. In our family, hors d'oeuvres are Jack Daniels with cashews, and dessert is Irish coffee. My parents are like, "Oh yeah, he's an alcoholic, ha ha." Like naming someone an alcoholic is no negative thing. We once went out with one of their friends for breakfast. It's 7:30 A.M. and he orders a Boilermaker, "just to level the playing field."

— *Julia Sweeney*

Students in Japan beat the heck out of American kids in important areas like science and math, and not acting like an idiot in public. That's because American kids, instead of studying, would rather spend their time in front of television sets that are made in, er . . . Japan.

— *Drew Carey*

God it'd be wild to be an Eskimo. Wouldn't it be cool to live in one of them icy igloos, get mad at one of your neighbors, go over and lick his house down?

— *Harland Williams*

My mom's your typical suburban Hindu. Just picture Donna Reed with a dot.

— *Shashi Bhatia*

Being Irish, I guess I should resent the Notre Dame nickname,"The Fighting Irish." After all, how long do you think nicknames like "The Bargaining Jews" or "The Murdering Italians" would last? Only the ironic Irish could be so naively honest. I get the feeling that Notre Dame came real close to naming itself "The Drunken, Thick-Skulled, Brawling, Short-Dicked Irish."

— *George Carlin*

I'm a defective Italian. I have absolutely no mechanical ability. You know when you go to the supermarket you step on that rubber part and the door opens? For years I thought that was a coincidence.

— *Richard Jeni*

It's dishonor if Japanese man is late. It means he has cheap watch.

— *Tamayo Otsuki*

I'm not typically Japanese, I'm very typically American—I'm lazy and I'm illiterate.

— *Bob Kubota*

I'm into Jewish bondage . . . that's having your money tied up in an IRA account.

— *Noodles Levenstein*

I was the only Jewish kid in my part of Indiana, and I'll never forget my kindergarten teacher asking, "So tell us, Hugh, how long has your family been practicing Jewcraft?"

— *Hugh Fink*

My father is a German Jew, and my mother is a French Jew. So that makes me—just really lucky to be here.

— *Jackie Wollner*

My mother is Jewish, my father Catholic. When I went to confession, I'd pray, "Bless me, father, for I have sinned. And I think you know my lawyer, Mr. Cohen."

— *Bill Maher*

Let me say something about the French. They look at us like we are one big collective Jethro bearing down on them. We might be hicks, but at least we're hicks who tend to our armpits more frequently than once every time the Comet Kahotec is in the solar system.

— *Dennis Miller*

I have two stepchildren. They're half Swedish and half Norwegian. They're see-through.

— *Cathy Ladman*

I'm a WASP, a white Anglo-Saxon Protestant, and actually, a lot of my people are doing really well.

— *Penelope Lombard*

Two reasons I don't think the Menendez brothers were really Latinos. One, we have a lot of respect for our parents and we'd never shoot them. Two, our parents would shoot back.

— *George Lopez*

I was walking down the street and this man actually calls me a Chink! I was so mad: Chinks are Chinese; I'm Korean—I'm a Gook. If you're going to be racist, at least get the terminology correct. Okay, Bubba?

— *Margaret Cho*

Evolution

I don't understand evolution. If we came from monkeys, why are there still monkeys? What, they couldn't make it over the hump? Pat Buchanan made it—what's up with their raggedy asses?

— *Kathleen Madigan*

Exercise

Aerobics: Gay folk dancing.

— *Bruce Smirnoff*

I got one of those Nordic tracks, and those are great. Although I hit a tree the other day.

— *Garry Shandling*

I'm all sore, because I got on the Stairmaster today and fell off it for about forty-five minutes.

— *Christopher Titus*

The only exercise program that has ever worked for me is occasionally getting up in the morning and jogging my memory to remind myself exactly how much I hate to exercise.

— *Dennis Miller*

My grandmother began walking five miles a day when she was eighty-two. Now we don't know where the hell she is.

— *Ellen DeGeneres*

Married people don't have to exercise, because our attitude is "They've seen us naked already—and they like it."

— *Carol Montgomery*

I can't work out in front of women. I don't want them to see me when I'm on my way to my goal—which is them!

— *Craig Shoemaker*

I don't exercise. If God wanted me to bend over, he would have put diamonds on the floor.

— *Joan Rivers*

I've been working out. I work out everything, except my ass. I don't work out my ass because I never think of it, I never see it. Unless something has gone horribly wrong. To me, it's a safety device to prevent me from falling in the toilet. So as long as it's doing its job, I don't have to make it look attractive, too. That's just a little too much pressure.

— *Garry Shandling*

You know, I really don't think I need buns of steel.
I'd be happy with buns of cinnamon.

— *Ellen DeGeneres*

I run, so I went to Footlocker in Hollywood and got
some Nike Cross Dressers, and I was halfway around
the track when heels popped out.

— *Garry Shandling*

Fame

I plan to be so successful, so famous, so well
respected that drag queens will want to dress like me
in parades when I'm dead.

— *Laura Kightlinger*

If you're famous over twenty minutes, you get your
own cologne.

— *Kim Castle*

Family

There were so many Wayans in our family, we had to
eat in alphabetical order.

— *Marlon Wayans*

My dad, he's a nuclear physicist, my mom, she's a mathematician, my brother is a chemical engineer—and I like to color.

— *Shashi Bhatia*

There's no such thing as fun for the whole family; there are no massage parlors with ice cream and free jewelry.

— *Jerry Seinfeld*

My family is so dysfunctional that if I had to write a song about them, it would be called, "Gimme, Ain't You Got, Loan Me, Don't You Have." It would be No. 1 on the country-western charts for weeks.

— *Paulara R. Hawkins*

In my house I learned at a very young age how to be a Jew. "If you're not miserable, you're not practicing." Oh, don't worry, I'm practicing.

— *Cynthia Levin*

My family is really boring. They have a coffee table book called *Pictures We Took Just to Use Up the Rest of the Film*.

— *Penelope Lombard*

I love my family, but I hate family reunions. Family reunions are that time when you come face to face with your family tree and realize some branches need to be cut.

— *Rene Hicks*

Fans

There's got to be something wrong with people who go to *Star Trek* conventions. I mean, I like M*ary Tyler Moore* too, but I don't rent out a big hall and dress up like Rhoda.

— *Andy Kindler*

Fashion

If the shoe fits, get another one just like it.

— *George Carlin*

Someone recently wrote a letter . . . "Why does Ellen DeGeneres always wear pants and never skirts?" . . . I had both of my legs completely tattooed with designs of bougainvillea. Now, if I wear a skirt, I am constantly bothered by bees.

— *Ellen DeGeneres*

Why does women's underwear have lace and flowers all over it? You never see men's underwear with a big wrench in the middle of it.

— *Heidi Joyce*

Eighteen-year-old kid, head shaved, both ears pierced, both nostrils pierced, both eyebrows pierced, tattoos coming out of the arms. He's got baggy pants that start at the knees, and twenty-seven inches of underwear. What's that about? That's one of the basic rules we know about—the underwear goes inside the pants! That's why it's called *Under*-fucking-wear.

— *Denis Leary*

On edible underwear: I don't know what the big deal is about these. You wear them for a couple of days, they taste just like the other ones.

— *Tom Arnold*

I got some new underwear the other day. Well, new to me.

— *Emo Philips*

I'm not ashamed of my body, I just don't see any reason to not cover it up as much as possible. I'm one of those people who think those garments the

Amish women wear are a great idea for everyone, regardless of their religious affiliation. I'm someone who considered becoming a nun, for the outfits.

— *Julia Sweeney*

Jesus was a cross-dresser.

— *George Carlin*

Fathers

My father looked at kids as additions to his tool kit. He got me, apparently, after thinking, "Oh, it's snowing again. I'll go back to bed and make a little snow-shoveling machine."

— *Bob Odenkirk*

My father wore the pants in the family—at least, after the court order.

— *Vernon Chatman*

My father is amazing. One day, he taught me something very valuable. He took me aside and passed down some of his wisdom. He said, "If, at the end of your life, you can count all of your friends—your really good friends—on just one hand, then you've been spending a lot of time alone in your room."

That's what he told me. And his hand was in his pants when he said it.

— *Bob Saget*

My father would say things that make no sense, like "If I were the last person on earth, some moron would turn left in front of me."

— *Louie Anderson*

My father heard the story of the Menendez brothers. He quit playing the lottery. He said, "Screw it. I've got twelve kids. Any one of them could snap."

— *Paul Rodriguez*

Forget low fat. My father used to take them hamburgers right off the grill, 95 percent fat, the other 5 percent lighter fluid.

— *Jack Coen*

My dad didn't like people as much as he liked his car. He even introduced it to people. "It's my Bonneville," he said. "My family's over there." Then he went on, "It's an American-made car. You can drive it head-on into a train and live." That was my cue to mutter, "You ought to try that, dad. The seven-fifteen's coming around the bend."

— *Louie Anderson*

I'm a grown woman but my father still thinks I know nothing about my car. He always asks me, "You changing the oil every 3,000?" "Yes, Dad. I'm also putting sugar in the gas tank. That way my exhaust smells like cotton candy."

— *Mimi Gonzalez*

My father was so cheap. We'd eat Hamburger Helper with no hamburger.

— *A.J. Jamal*

My dad's so cheap. He's always yelling at me for spending money. "Look at you, spending money, you're such a big shot." Oh, yeah, buying food, paying rent. I'm just showing off.

— *Cathy Ladman*

My father was so cheap that one year he told us Santa didn't come because he wears red and we lived in a Crips zone.

— *A.J. Jamal*

My father refused to spend money on me as a kid. One time I broke my arm playing football and my father tried to get a free X ray by taking me down to the airport and making me lie down with the luggage.

— *Glen Super*

They say when you die there's a light at the end of the tunnel. When my father dies, he'll see the light, make his way toward it, and then flip it off to save electricity.

— *Harland Williams*

My father used to ground me—and then run electricity through me.

— *Taylor Negron*

I remember when I was a teenager taking the car for a night out, sometimes my dad would take me aside and say, "Son, here's an extra $271. Treat yourself to a car pool lane violation."

— *Bil Dwyer*

My dad's hearing is gone and he won't admit it. When he reads, he goes "What?" The mind is slowly following. He called me up the other night, very excited. He says, "Jonathan, when I get up to go to the bathroom in the middle of the night I don't have to turn on the light, the light goes on automatically. When I'm done, the light goes off automatically." I said, "Dad, you're peeing in the fridge, and it's got to stop."

— *Jonathan Katz*

Fathers are the geniuses of the house because only a person as intelligent as we could fake such stupidity. Think about your father: He doesn't know where anything is. You ask him to do something, he messes it up, and your mother sends you: "Go down and see what your father's doing before he blows up the house." He's a genius at work because he doesn't want to do it, and knows someone will be coming soon to stop him.

— *Bill Cosby*

Something happens when a man reaches a certain age, that The News becomes the most important thing in his life. All fathers think one day they're going to get a call from the State Department. "Listen, we've completely lost track of the situation in the Middle East. You've been watching the news. What do you think we should do about it?"

— *Jerry Seinfeld*

What is it with dads? They turn forty or fifty and they become Mr. Fix It. You find 'em nude cruising around the house with a screwdriver in one hand. "I'm gonna tighten something."

— *Gary Barkin*

My dad's pants kept creeping up on him. By sixty-five he was just a pair of pants and a head.

— *Jeff Altman*

"Don't get smart with me," my father would growl. That was my favorite expression of his. Don't get smart with me. Just once I wanted to make a weird face and go, "Duh! Is this dumb enough for you, Dad?"

— *Louie Anderson*

My father listens to AM radio really loud. There's no reason for that.

— *Shashi Bhatia*

My dad, eighty-six years old and he's still working, God bless him. He's a pimp, and he's out there every night.

— *Jonathan Katz*

Fear

My biggest irrational fear is of being kidnapped—but that's so very seventies, so Chowcilla. I know that if I'm going to be afraid, it should be a more up-to-date, timely fear—like being shot in a drive-by, or murdered by a tacky, high school vampire cult that works out of a minivan.

— *Dorothea Coelho*

Feminist

When I say I'm a feminist, I make it clear I'm not anti-male, just anti-asshole. Having been an asshole myself, I realize that it's a gender-free concept.

— *Mimi Gonzalez*

I wanted to be a feminist in high school, but my boyfriend wouldn't let me.

— *Denis Munro Robb*

Rush Limbaugh calls feminists "feminazis." But having Rush Limbaugh call you a Nazi is like having Kato Kaelin call you a freeloader.

— *Jackie Wollner*

Fishing

We're fishing and my wife had a problem with killing the fish. I wasn't crazy with that part either, but I figured, if we just wait for them to die naturally, it could take forever. Certainly till after supper.

— *Paul Reiser*

Fire

I remember the day the candle shop burned down. Everyone just stood around and sang Happy Birthday.

— *Steven Wright*

Florida

I like Florida; everything is in the eighties: the temperature, the ages, and the IQs.

— *George Carlin*

My parents moved to Florida—they didn't want to, but they're in their sixties, and that's the law.

— *Jerry Seinfeld*

Flying

I'm afraid of planes—I don't trust the oxygen mask. The little orange cup—attached to that bag that's full of nothing. Maybe I'm cynical. I don't even think that it's an oxygen mask. I think it's more to just muffle the screams.

— *Rita Rudner*

There ought to be an FAA requirement that crying babies have to go into the overhead compartment.

— *Bobby Slayton*

Limited carry-on—the stewardess said your carry-on bag had to fit in the ass of the passenger in front of you.

— *Dennis Miller*

The Concorde was great. It travels at twice the speed of sound. Which is fun except you can't hear the movie until two hours after you land.

— *Howie Mandel*

The airlines banned smoking on their flights. Now if they can do it on their landings. . . .

— *Barry Crimmins*

The nicest thing about a plane crashing at an air show is that they always have good video of the actual crash.

— *George Carlin*

I flew in one of these little-bitty-ass planes—it was playing Buddy Holly music. I'm like, "Can we change the station or something, man!" They didn't have any departure schedule or arrival schedule or nothin'. They didn't even have an intercom. They were just outside, "We're leaving! Bring your ass, we're leaving!"

— *Jamie Foxx*

Some people have the audacity to put a little bolt through their penis. Which makes me think it must be fun at the airport metal detector. "Will you take out your keys? Do you have any other metal on you? Yes? Will you take that out, too?"

— *Robin Williams*

We don't know how old the airplanes are and there's really no way for us to tell, 'cause we're laymen. But I figure if the plane smells like your grandmother's house, get out. That's where I draw the line.

— *Garry Shandling*

The flight attendant will always tell you the name of your pilot. Like anyone goes, "Oh, he's good. I like his work."

— *David Spade*

Food

I'm addicted to chocolate—I used to snort cocoa.

— *Marilyn*

McDonald's "breakfast for under a dollar" actually costs much more than that. You have to factor in the cost of coronary bypass surgery.

— *George Carlin*

In Europe they use all the parts of the animal we throw away. Look in their dumpsters; there's the prime rib. They're saving the lungs and the pancreas for some kind of colon tartar.

— *Jay Leno*

Nobody says, "Can I have your beets?"

— *Bill Cosby*

I look at rice cakes and think, Who woke up one morning and said, "Packing material, pressed into a disc, yummmmm"? A friend puts jam on rice cakes and considers it dessert. You could put Madonna on a rice cake, and I would still choose ice cream.

— *Sabrina Matthews*

I never eat sushi. I have trouble eating things that are merely unconscious.

— *George Carlin*

The formula for water is H_2O. Is the formula for an ice cube H_2O squared?

— *Lily Tomlin*

I saw a product in the market, Mr. Salty Pretzels. Isn't that nerve? Everything nowadays is low salt or salt-free. Here's a guy, the hell with you, Mr. Salty Pretzels. Like Mr. Tar and Nicotine Cigarettes, Mr. Gristle and Hard Artery Beefsteak.

— *Bill Maher*

I bought some powdered water, but I don't know what to add.

— *Steven Wright*

A government report says raw eggs may have salmonella, and may be unsafe. In fact, the latest government theory says it wasn't the fall that killed Humpty Dumpty—he was dead before he hit the ground.

— *Jay Leno*

Frankenstein

Frankenstein was a strange monster. As a kid, I never understood him. He never caught any black people. No Mexicans either. He only went after very scared white people. He never went into the ghetto. A black guy with Nikes would have run circles around his ass. "Yeah, come on, Frankie, bring your green ass over here." If Frankenstein went into the barrio, the Mexicans would've taken those bolts right out of his head. "Well, thanks, man. We need that shit for our tires. I'm glad you showed up, man. My wheel was loose."

— *Paul Rodriguez*

Friend

I hate the expression "A friend is a present you give yourself." Gag. A case of Heineken is a present you give yourself. A friend is someone you don't have to talk to once there's food on the table.

— *Sabrina Matthews*

You need to have a stupid girlfriend so that on a bad day you can call her. "Tanya, I'm having a bad day, tell me something stupid you've done. You caught on fire, and you tried to put it out with alcohol?"

— *Ellen Cleghorne*

Gangs

My homeboy Tito was always trying to get me to join a gang. Tito, with two black eyes, arm in a sling, and crutches, saying, "Hey Willie, why don't you join the gang—you get protection!"

— *Willie Barcena*

Gardening

Gardening is so complex. I can only grow simple plants, like mildew. My friend has a green thumb. She makes salad—it takes root. She has a hedge made out of broccoli.

— *Jeannie Dietz*

Gay

Using the word "gay" as a euphemism for homosexual is fine, I guess. But I've always thought a word like "fabulous" might have been better. Sure would be a lot easier to tell your parents, "Mom, Dad—I'm *fabulous!* And my friends are fabulous, too!"

— *Michael Greer*

My high school had a Head Start program for homo-sexuals—it was called Drama Club.

— *Bob Smith*

Hillary Clinton says it takes a village to raise a child. Which I think is nice, but for a gay person it takes the Village People.

— *Jason Stuart*

Gay men look at fidelity differently than everyone else. With fags, it's not called cheating unless you're actually playing cards.

— *Scott Thompson*

My parents were in denial about my being gay. I wasn't afraid of the dark, I was afraid of unflattering light.

— *Bob Smith*

Gay Republicans—how exactly does that work? "We disapprove of our own lifestyle. We beat ourselves up in parking lots."

— *Paula Poundstone*

People think you're a lesbian because you can't get a man. Then explain to me why the only times in my life I've slept with men was when I couldn't get a woman.

— *Georgia Ragsdale*

Most parents of gay children are unprepared to give them guidance. It's not advisable for a lesbian daughter to try to use her father's method of keeping a woman happy: Agree to whatever she says, and then do what you want anyway.

— *Bob Smith*

Straight people are fine—I have one of them fix my car. They do great work.

— *Michael Rasky*

The heterosexuals who hate us should just stop having us.

— *Lynda Montgomery*

Strange times we live in. A town in Florida with a street named Gay Avenue is changing its name because a resident says people automatically thought he was gay. He wants the new name of the street to be I Ain't No Homo Lane.

— *Conan O'Brien*

There's this town in the midwest called Dyke. Women on their way to the Michigan Womyn's Festival stop to have their pictures taken at the Dyke city limits sign. Apparently, the citizens of Dyke don't appreciate this yearly pilgrimage. But if they don't want us to visit, just change the name of the town to Uptight Straight White Guy—we'll stay away.

— *Sabrina Matthews*

Oprah Winfrey issued a statement saying that even though she appeared on the *Ellen* coming-out episode, she's not gay. Meanwhile, Ellen DeGeneres issued a statement saying even though she appeared on *Oprah,* she's not black.

— *Conan O'Brien*

Any supposedly Christian doctrine must have at the core a belief in the concept of unqualified love for your fellow man. There's no version of the Bible that says Love Thy Neighbor—unless he's a Peter Allen fan.

— *Dennis Miller*

Glasses

My mother got her cataracts removed several years ago. The doctor gave her these huge sunglasses to wear. She still wears them. She thinks they are attractive. She looks like Bea Arthur as a welder.

— *Judy Gold*

Some people have a lot of vanity. They say, "I only wear glasses when I drive." If you only need glasses when you drive, why not drive around with a prescription windshield!

— *Brian Regan*

Yesterday I was walking down the street wearing my eyeglasses and all of a sudden my prescription ran out.

— *Steven Wright*

I wear glasses, primarily so I can look for the things that I keep losing.

— *Bill Cosby*

My girlfriend just got glasses, and I think I'm in trouble. I heard her upstairs looking in the mirror and saying, "Wait a minute—I'm a model! Bye."

— *Chris Mancini*

God

The philosopher Pascal said you had to bet that there was a God or there wasn't, but you couldn't avoid the wager. Kind of like a cosmic *Let's Make a Deal:* Do you want to have fun in this life?—or trade it for what's behind the final curtain?

— *Frank Miles*

I pray twice a day, but I often say something mean to God.

— *Mike McDonald*

Let's face it. God has a big ego problem. Why do we always have to worship Him? "Oh, you're the greatest. You're perfect. We're fuck-ups. You know everything. We're in the dark." Secure people don't need to hear that all the time.

— *Bill Maher*

If I ever get the chance, I have a couple of questions I want to ask God, and it's not the usual "Why is there suffering?" I'd like to know what was the biggest, grossest bug that ever crawled on anyone, but they didn't notice, and then it crawled away.

— *Julia Sweeney*

If God loves us all so much, how come he never makes rain taste minty? So everyone can have fresh breath. Well, Bob, he has more important things to do, there are people starving to death, after all. Yes! I know! I'm thinking of them! Especially starving people—you know how bad your breath gets when you haven't eaten a thing in weeks?

— *Bob Odenkirk*

I wonder why God didn't give us wheels? He must have known we'd get skates for Christmas.

— *Gallagher*

Good Old Days

I was at a party where somebody was talking about the Good Old Days. I was like, "Which Good Old Days? During the McCarthy blacklist? Or when blacks couldn't vote? When they burned women at the stake because they were herbalists? Those Good Old Days?"

— *Beth Lapides*

Grandparents

My grandparents gave me Scratch and Cough books when I was growing up, Scene of the Accident coloring books.

— *Richard Lewis*

My grandfather lived to be 103 years old. The truth is, nobody knows what's good for you. Every morning he would eat an entire raw onion and smoke a cigar. You know what his dying words were? Nobody knows, they couldn't get near the guy.

— *Jonathan Katz*

My grandfather was in this Russian, this Yiddish circus. He was a Jewish juggler. He used to worry about six things at once.

— *Richard Lewis*

I played with my grandfather a lot when I was a kid. He was dead, but my parents had him cremated and put his ashes in my Etch-a-Sketch.

— *Alan Havey*

"Don't worry about senility," my grandfather used to say. "When it hits you, you won't know it."

— *Bill Cosby*

I've been storing my grandmother in Florida, but now I want to move her north to cooler weather. I figure she'll keep better, and maybe that phlegm will break up. Each morning she's in the bathroom for two hours making grotesque guttural noises. Sounds like she's making espresso. She called yesterday to say she'd gone to the beauty parlor. I said, "Well, it's your money."

— *Larry Amoros*

My grandmother, who's in her nineties, she still drives. People hear that and say, "God love her." But no one will get in the car with her. "No, we don't need a ride, Ada. We'll just hitchhike." She has a 1962 Dodge Dart, it has the push-button transmission. At this point it's like a damn slot machine. She's hit so many motorcycles, there are stencils of motorcycles painted on the side of the car.

— *Garry Shandling*

Gun Control

This country loves guns, we even have salad shooters. This country thinks that salad is too peaceable, you have to find some way to shoot it.

— *Bill Maher*

The Second Amendment gave us the right to bear arms in order to have a ready militia. It's not for traffic incidents.

— *Paula Poundstone*

Congress voted against a proposal to have a national seven-day waiting period to buy a gun. Is a week a long time to wait? To see if a former mental patient is qualified to own an Uzi? Come on, it takes three weeks to get a phone!

— *Jimmy Tingle*

Remember, kids, guns aren't for fun. Guns are for killing things like songbirds, and deer, and intruders, and mailboxes, and Spice Girls, and busybodies who just won't leave your cult alone, and women who don't understand you're the best man for them. That may sound crazy, but when you're holding a gun, you decide who's crazy. 'Cause kids, remember, guns don't kill people—unless you practice real hard.

— *Bill Maher*

Virginia has passed a law limiting people to the purchase of one gun per person per month. But if you can show the need for more than one gun a month, you can apply to the police for an exemption. "Listen, officer, we've got a really dysfunctional family here, and . . . "

— *George Carlin*

The FBI recently released the information that most of the guns in New York City came from five southern states. The rest came from the backseat of a car owned by the Wutan clan.

— *Colin Quinn*

Please people, if you don't have a gun, for God's sake go out and get one. Because you never know when you're gonna be downtown someday, it's cold and dark, and all of a sudden you're gonna need some money.

— *Harland Williams*

The NRA has their cute little bumper sticker, "You'll get my gun when you pry it from my cold dead hands." Whatever. In a perfect world.

— *Dennis Miller*

What's with the NRA? They don't want to outlaw automatic weapons. I guess you have to understand where they're coming from. They feel it's okay to shoot a human, as long as you eat the meat after.

— *Elayne Boosler*

Gynecologists

I got a postcard from my gynecologist. It said, "Did you know it's time for your annual check-up?" No. But now my mailman does. Why don't you just send me a Petrie dish while you're at it?

— *Cathy Ladman*

Having a male gynecologist is like going to an auto mechanic who doesn't own a car.

— *Carrie Snow*

h i j k

Hair

The hairier the person, the smaller the bikini underwear they have on. I can't figure it out.

— *Paul Rodriguez*

If I don't tweeze every day, my eyebrows need barrettes.

— *Nancy Mura*

I guess I'm sensitive about my hair loss. I think everybody's making fun of it. I went to buy a VCR, the guy said, "Four head?"—and I beat the hell out of him.

— *Dan Wilson*

I get a lot of clients with unreasonable expectations of what a hairdresser can accomplish. They want to look like *Friends,* and the closest I can get them is *Acquaintances*. Or maybe, *Enemies*.

— *Le Maire*

This is the kind of thing would bum out any young guy. I just found out my father lost his hair—in a slap fight.

— *Vernon Chatman*

I got to see Don King up close, and even as a woman I don't know how you get your hair to do that all the time. I guess one day you walk into a barber shop and say, "I want to look as though I'm falling out of a building." And then pull a little troll doll out of your pocket, "This is the look I'm shooting for."

— *Kathleen Madigan*

I dye my hair so much, my driver's license has a color wheel.

— *Nancy Mura*

Handicapped

I'm proud to be handicapped. If it weren't for me, you'd be spending all day looking for a place to park.

— *Gene Mitchner*

I was born with a club foot. Had to wear orthopedic shoes with a heel this thick on one side and a brace, so I used to walk with a limp. Thank God I lived in the ghetto, because the people who didn't know me thought I was cool, "Hey man, check out this brother's walk, he must be in a gang or something."

— *Damon Wayans*

Recently, in a public bathroom, I used the handicapped stall. As I emerged, a man in a wheelchair asked me indignantly, "Are you handicapped?" Gathering all my aplomb, I looked him in the eye and said, "Not now. But I was before I went in there."

— *George Carlin*

I was in a school for the retarded for two years, before they found out I was hearing impaired. And they called me slow!

— *Kathy Buckley*

I have cerebral palsy, and I don't understand why people will go out of their way to drink so they walk like me.

— *Geri Jewell*

Harass

I hate these guys who harass women on the street. It's not even a compliment. They'll harass bag ladies.

"Hey, baby. I'd like to see what's under that third coat."

— Dom Irrera

I really hate it when strange men on the street say, "Smile! You'd look so much prettier if you'd smile." I always feel like saying, "Get hard! You'd look so much more useful if you had an erection."

— Cathryn Michon

Health

I had a cholesterol test: They found bacon.

— Bob Zany

There is something refreshingly ironic about people lying on the beach contracting skin cancer in an attempt to acquire a purely illusory appearance of good health, while germ-laden medical waste washes up on the sand all around them.

— George Carlin

I worry about my health because I grew up on the tail end of the baby boom generation, and we were just pumped full of chemicals. Every time they came up with a new one, it was like,"Put it on the cereal, keep it crunchy. Hey, put out the light, my teeth are glowing!" Now my whole generation is eating tree bark to clean ourselves out.

— *Jack Coen*

I take geranium, dandelion, passionflower, hibiscus—I feel great, and when I pee, I experience the fresh scent of potpourri.

— *Sheila Wenz*

I had a heart attack. Your heart get mad, "Think about dying now, ain't you? You didn't think about it when you was eating that pork."

— *Richard Pryor*

I take vitamins. They drop and roll under the refrigerator. I don't pick them up. I have years of vitamins under the refrigerator. I'm going to come home one night and find a six-foot roach saying, "I feel good!"

— *Elayne Boosler*

I had a chest X ray last month, and they found a spot on my lung. Fortunately, it was barbecue sauce.

— *George Carlin*

Heights

A lot of people are afraid of heights. Not me—I'm afraid of widths.

— *Steven Wright*

Hobby

I have a large seashell collection, which I keep scattered on beaches all over the world.

— *Steven Wright*

Holidays

All religions are the same: basically guilt, with different holidays. "I feel so guilty. Well, let's eat."

— *Cathy Ladman*

My father was a separatist black Muslim. When Santa at the mall asked me what I wanted, my father shouted, "Tell him you want your freedom! Got any freedom in that bag, fat man?" And I thought I'd wanted some Rock 'em Sock 'em Robots.

— *Warren Hutcherson*

Jesus never put up a tree and exchanged gifts, or left cookies out for Santa. He never made a harried last-minute trip to the mall, or spent Christmas Eve cursing at a toy that he couldn't put together. He celebrated Passover. So, if you want to be more like Jesus, pass the matzo.

— *Drew Carey*

The Supreme Court has ruled they cannot have a nativity scene in Washington, D.C. This wasn't for any religious reasons. They couldn't find three wise men and a virgin.

— *Jay Leno*

Probably the worst thing about being Jewish during Christmastime is shopping, because the lines are so long. They should have a Jewish express line: "Look, I'm a Jew, it's not a gift. It's just paper towels!"

— *Sue Kolinsky*

Fat Tuesday is an annual event in New Orleans in which Roman Catholics eat, drink, and run wild. On the other 364 nights of the year, the event is held in Hyannisport.

— *Argus Hamilton*

Christmas is not really my holiday, being neither a Christian nor a toy manufacturer. And although clinical depression is scary, I'm not any more depressed during the holidays than usual—the other day I actually had a Near Life Experience.

— *Mark Shapiro*

Los Angeles can be dark and confusing. During the holidays I went to the mall and sat on Satan's lap.

— *Leslie Nesbitt*

My father was so cheap. For Easter, we'd wear the same clothes, but he'd take us to a different church.

— *A.J. Jamal*

I have these two lesbian friends in L.A.—they're having a kid, they're going to a sperm bank. But I like to torture them. I called them up the other day and said, "What are you going to do for Father's Day, go out to dinner with the turkey baster?"

— *Judy Gold*

Evangelists say Halloween is the devil's holiday. What a lame-ass devil! Sitting down in the depths of hell, going, "I've got control of the major corporations, churning out weapons and toxic waste, but how can I get *candy?* Let me think—I'll get the children of the world to dress up as hobos and Power Rangers—and then I'll have all the bite-size Three Musketeers I need! I am Satan!"

— Patton Oswalt

This is the first year that Wall Street took off for Martin Luther King Day. That shows you something, 'cause there are some conservative guys there. But Martin Luther King Day is also honored at banks, schools, the post office, and a tiny four-inch patch of Michael Jackson.

— Bill Maher

In Hollywood, children don't wear masks on Halloween. They usually dress up as agents, valet parkers, or second-unit directors instead.

— Ellen DeGeneres

I'm glad that Hanukkah's over, because I never know what to get my parents. Last year I bought them a gift certificate for Dr. Kevorkian. So I didn't think this year would be a problem, but I guess they forgot to look at the expiration date.

— Cathy Ladman

When I was little I asked my mother, "Do you love me?" She said, "I love you when you're sleeping."

When I was fourteen, I asked, "Mom, am I ugly?" She said, "It's okay, when you're sixteen you can get a nose job." When I was leaving for school, she said, "I don't know why we're spending any money to send you to college—you don't deserve it." When I came home for Mother's Day, she asked, "Where's my present?" I said, "Your present is—I still only have one personality—and it's not planning to kill you!"

— *Robin Roberts*

At Thanksgiving, my mom always makes too much food, especially one item, like 700 or 800 pounds of sweet potatoes. She's got to push it during the meal. "Did you get some sweet potatoes? . . . They're hot. There's more in the oven . . . some more in the garage. The rest are at the Johnsons'."

— *Louie Anderson*

There's a lot of New York City Thanksgiving traditions. For example, a lot of New Yorkers don't buy the frozen Thanksgiving turkey. They prefer to buy the bird live and then push it in front of a subway train.

— *David Letterman*

The Jews don't have any little animated characters. I think their religion could catch on more commercially if, you know, the Hanukah raccoon, the Passover turtle . . . something.

— *Paula Poundstone*

New Year's Eve, where auld acquaintance be forgot. Unless, of course, those tests come back positive.

— *Jay Leno*

Homeless

I always give homeless people money, and my friends yell at me, "He's only going to buy more alcohol and cigarettes." And I'm thinking, "Oh, and like I wasn't?"

— *Kathleen Madigan*

The worst thing about being homeless is that you'll never be able to enjoy camping. If you don't believe me, ask a homeless person. "Hey, pal, you want to go to Yosemite? Sleep under the stars tonight?" "No, fuck you. Take me home."

— *Paul Rodriguez*

We used to drive by the homeless and wonder what we could do to help. Now we say, "Lock the doors." I think most people would rather help them. But these days you can't even suggest it. You're driving by a homeless guy and say, "Should we pick that guy up?" "No, he could get up if he wanted to." "But he's only got one leg." "Well, he shouldn't have fallen down then, should he?"

— *Louie Anderson*

Rush Limbaugh and his ilk think the homeless are just the weakest of the herd who should be sent off to the Island of Misfit Toys without a pang of remorse. Ironically enough, Limbaugh is very popular with the homeless community, 'cause there always seems to be a new refrigerator box in his trash bin.

— *Dennis Miller*

I would do anything for the homeless. Give them money. Whatever. You know why? Because I don't want them moving into my house.

— *Paul Rodriguez*

Home Furnishing

Guys learn this: even if you're just living with a woman you're not even married to —give up any thought of being involved in interior decoration of the place you're going to live in. All your beer stuff, your sports mirrors, put them in storage—you're only going to visit them occasionally. I've been to Wayne Gretsky's house, he's got five MVP trophies, and you know where they are? They're in the fucking garage.

— *Denis Leary*

I filled out a rental application that asked, "Do you own any liquid-filled furniture?" Couldn't they just have said "waterbed"? How many other forms of liquid-filled furniture are there? "Yeah, I have a beer couch, will that be a problem?"

— *Lisa Goich*

I wanted to buy some carpeting, you know how much they want for carpeting? Fifteen dollars a square yard! And I'm sorry, I'm not going to pay that for carpeting. So what I did, I bought two square yards, and when I go home I strap them to my feet.

— *Steve Martin*

My mother wrapped the living room furniture in plastic. We practiced safe sitting in our household.

— *Adam Ferrara*

I have a little house in L.A. It's nice. Well, the bedroom is nice. I have French doors in the bedroom. They don't open unless I lick them.

— *Judy Gold*

Remember when Michael Jackson wanted to buy the remains of the Elephant Man? What was he thinking? Let's see: Michael was walking around his palace going, "In that corner, I just don't know. A palm tree, an end table, naw . . . a dead guy! Yeah, that's it."

— *Paul Rodriguez*

Honesty

Honesty may be the best policy, but it's important to remember that apparently, by elimination, dishonesty is the second-best policy.

— *George Carlin*

Honesty is the best policy, but insanity is a better defense.

— *Steve Landesberg*

Housework

Why do they put lights on vacuum cleaners? To see the dirt? I don't want to see the dirt, that's why I vacuum.

— *Jeannie Dietz*

I never get tired of housework—I don't do any. When guests come to visit, I just put out dropcloths and say we're painting.

— *Joan Rivers*

My mother used to say, "You can eat off my floor." You can eat off my floor, too. There's thousands of things there.

— *Elayne Boosler*

Humor

Men always say the most important thing in a woman is a sense of humor. You know what that means? He's looking for someone to laugh at *his* jokes.

— *Sheila Wenz*

Women claim that what they look for in a man is a sense of humor, but I don't believe it. Who do you want removing your bra—Tom Selleck or the Three Stooges?

— *Bruce Smirnoff*

Hunting

Do you know how the Amish hunt? They sneak up on a deer and build a barn around it.

— *Tim Bedore*

You ask people why they have deer heads on the wall. They say, "Because it's such a beautiful animal." I think my mother's attractive, but I have photographs of her.

— *Ellen DeGeneres*

Husbands

All wives give their husbands what's known as the "retardo" job. It's basically a simple task, that when you screw it up, they know they can fix it anyway. They just want to see if you're smarter than, say, an onion.

— *Tim Monahan*

They think it's your destiny to clean, and I guess it's their destiny to have a couch surgically implanted on their behind. You may marry the man of your dreams, ladies, but years later you're married to a couch that burps.

— *Roseanne*

My ex-husband was a drummer, and he had this nervous habit of hitting on things—like my girlfriends. Yeah, he was always banging on something.

— *Le Maire*

I have to talk to my girlfriend every day on the phone. My husband says, "Why do you have to talk to her again today? You just talked to her yesterday. What could you possibly have to tell her?" "Well, for one thing, I have to tell her you just said that."

— *Rita Rudner*

Immigration

All the problems we face in the United States today can be traced to an unenlightened immigration policy on the part of the American Indian.

— *Pat Paulsen*

Since the Indians got swindled over some beads, nobody in America has been too excited about newcomers. Every racial and ethnic group gets treated like shit when they get here—by the racial and ethnic group that got treated like shit when they came in on the earlier flight. Nobody says, "Hey, here are the new guys. Let's welcome them. Let's bake a cake for the Irish."

— *Chris Rock*

Impotence

The latest news on this new impotency drug Viagra. Some insurance companies won't pay unless men can prove that they're impotent. Which means that men are at a disadvantage if they have a really hot pharmacist.

— *Conan O'Brien*

Inconsiderate

I'm getting more and more inconsiderate. I slept with a young guy and afterward I said, "That was fun. It's been so long since I've slept with someone for a ride home."

— *Laura Kightlinger*

Inspiration

Some people see things that are and ask, Why? Some people dream of things that never were and ask, Why not? Some people have to go to work and don't have time for all that shit.

— *George Carlin*

Insurance

All the big stars from my parents' generation are on cable selling things. Like Ed McMahon. My mom and dad loved him. Now he's selling insurance policies to the elderly, asking them to send in $7.95 out of their last $8 for a policy that will leave money to children who don't visit them.

— *Louie Anderson*

My wife and I took out life insurance policies on one another—so now it's just a waiting game.

— *Bil Dwyer*

Intercourse

We were once having foreplay and she asked, "What's next?" She finally consented to having intercourse if she could combine it with learning a trade. And when we finally were screwing, she complained I was blocking her view.

— *Richard Lewis*

Intimacy

Here would be my Valentine's card that I think I'm gonna send to my boyfriend, "Things have been going so well thus far, I will find more ways to become unavailable to you."

— *Janeane Garofalo*

My girlfriend is not a ball and chain—she's more of a spring-loaded trap.

— *Kevin Hench*

I have a tremendous fear of intimacy. I feel lucky just to get aroused, because my penis is usually in the shape of a question mark. If I am lucky enough to get an erection, fortunately for me, my hard-on points to the nearest counseling center.

— *Richard Lewis*

Jealousy

Men get jealous more often, but women when they do go demented sometimes, and for weird reasons. I never thought that until I got married, and one day my wife came home from work and was mad at me because there was a pretty woman on the bus she thought I would have liked. "You bastard, you're horrible."

— *Ray Romano*

Jeopardy

If people on *Jeopardy* are so smart, then why can't they write their names better?

— *Todd Glass*

Jobs

The easiest job in the world has to be coroner. You perform surgery on dead people. What's the worst that could happen? If everything went wrong, maybe you'd get a pulse.

— *Dennis Miller*

One time I tried getting a job at a submarine sandwich shop. Only they wanted me to take a lie detector test just in order to apply for the job. What the hell am I going to lie about in a sub shop? Did they fear someone would ask for roast beef and I'd say no? "How much is the tuna?" "Thousands."

— *Paula Poundstone*

I was an accountant. I wasn't a very good accountant. I always felt that if you got within two or three bucks of it, that was close enough.

— *Bob Newhart*

I was a stewardess for a while on a helicopter. For about five or six people, tops. I'd ask, "Would you like something to drink? You would? Then we're going to have to land."

— *Rita Rudner*

I was on a job interview, and was asked what my dream job would be. I said, "The words 'dream' and 'job' don't really go together for me. How about 'dream, no job.' Do you have that?"

— *Chris Mancini*

It's so humiliating to go on job interviews, especially when they ask, "What was the reason you left your last job?" "Well, I found that after I was fired there was a lot of tension in the office. You know, I found it difficult sitting on the new girl's lap."

— *Caroline Rhea*

Justice

I don't think juries stand a chance with these slick lawyers. If justice is blind, maybe it's because lawyers are jerking it off.

— *Dennis Miller*

Kids

Hey, kids! It's mostly bullshit and garbage and none of the stuff they tell you is true. And when your dumb-ass father says he wants you to amount to something, he means make a lot of money. How do you think the word "amount" got in there?

— *George Carlin*

Kids? It's like living with homeless people. They're cute but they just chase you around all day long going, "Can I have a dollar? I'm missing a shoe! I need a ride!"

— *Kathleen Madigan*

Kids, they're not easy, but there has to be some penalty for sex.

— *Bill Maher*

We've begun to long for the pitter-patter of little feet—so we bought a dog. Well, it's cheaper, and you get more fcct.

— *Rita Rudner*

I want to get married and have a lot of kids. I figure the more wage-earning people I bear, the better my chances are of someday getting into a really good nursing home.

— *Brenda Pontiff*

I don't have any kids. Well, at least none that I know about. I'd like to have kids one day, though. I want to be called Mommy by someone other than Spanish guys in the street.

— *Carol Leifer*

I've been married fourteen years and I have three kids. Obviously, I breed well in captivity.

— *Roseanne*

When I was a kid, I was so short I had to blow my nose through my fly.

— *Rodney Dangerfield*

I remember when I first got my foster son. He was the cutest little guy I'd seen in my life. As I changed him, I was surprised by how much I liked it. I knew that I'd do what needed to be done. But there was always that little voice in the back of my head that said, "Remember, the saxophone was in the closet after a month."

— *Paula Poundstone*

Bruce Springsteen has kids and now he doesn't give any more of those four-hour concerts. After an hour and a half, he says, "Are you ready to rock and roll?" And the audience answers, "No, Bruce, we've got sitters." And he says, "Oh, shit, me, too. Goodnight."

— *Paul Clay*

The only way my wife and I could afford to have kids is if she breast-fed them for eighteen years.

— *Paul Alexander*

You have kids—kids will mess you up. You sit there and say, "My parents are goofy." You made them that way.

— *Sinbad*

I have two-year-old twins in my house, it's nuts. I make excuses to get out: "You need anything from anywhere? Anything from the Motor Vehicle Bureau? C'mon, let me register something. I was going out anyway, to apply for jury duty. Please!"

— *Ray Romano*

Kids are cute, babies are cute, puppies are cute. The little things are cute. See, nature did this on purpose so that we would want to take care of our young. Made them cute. Tricked us. Then gradually they get older and older, until one day your mother sits you down and says, "You know, I think you're ugly enough to get your own apartment."

— *Cathy Ladman*

My friends ask is there a difference between having a son or a daughter. No doubt about it, the day my daughter was born everyone began to look like a potential molester to me. "Ho, ho, ho, my ass—she's not sitting on your lap."

— *Jack Coen*

When you were a little kid, remember how hard it was to get a cookie? Way in the back, unless your mom was really mean—then they'd be on top of the refrigerator. Nowhere, anyplace on a package of Oreos does it say, "Keep out of reach of small children." Where's the Liquid Drano? Under the sink, right next to the rest of the poisons.

— *Mike Bullard*

I was in McDonald's and I saw this kid take his Happy Meal toy and throw it on the ground. His mom said, "Hey, you play with that. There are children in China who are manufacturing those."

— *Laura Silverman*

I've got good kids . . . love my kids. I'm trying to bring them up the right way, not spanking them. I find waving the gun around gets the same job done.

— *Denis Leary*

My goddaughter is so cute. She's two and a half. She saw her father in the shower and she came running out screaming, "Mommy, daddy has a tail!" Of course, I'm the evil single girl, I had to ask, "Is it a big tail?" Mommy's lucky.

— *Caroline Rhea*

When we watched *Peter Pan* my six-year-old came up with a beautiful question. "Daddy, how does Captain Hook wipe himself?" That was so sweet. My first thought was to tell her that he just rips himself a new asshole. But, "Smee does it," I told her.

— *Bob Saget*

Kindergarten

Did you ever read that book *Everything I Needed to Know I Learned in Kindergarten*? I learned only two things in kindergarten: First, if someone has something you want, you can remove it from them physically. And second, Elmer's glue makes a great between-meals snack.

— *Gary Barkin*

Las Vegas

I just got back from Vegas and I have a suggestion for all the casinos: When a cocktail waitress reaches the age of sixty, let her wear pants.

— *Chris Mancini*

Land

I bought some land. It was kind of cheap. It was on somebody else's property.

— *Steven Wright*

Language

I'm learning to speak Spanish by calling my bank and pressing the #2 button.

— *Paul Alexander*

I would love to speak a foreign language but I can't. So I grew hair under my arms instead.

— *Sue Kolinsky*

Laundry

You know it's time to do the laundry when you dry off with a sneaker.

— *Zach Galifianakis*

Law

Few people realize that Shakespeare once studied law. The original working title of *King Lear* was actually *Estate Planning: A Trouble-Shooting Guide for the Wealthy Land Owner.*

— *Brenda Pontiff*

The frightening reality is every day this society seems to make its legal decisions in much the same way the Archies picked their vacation spots—blindfold Jughead, give him a dart, and spin the globe.

— *Dennis Miller*

Leather

Leather jackets scare me. Think about it, people are wearing dried meat for clothing. They're spending $500 to wear beef jerky.

— *Brad Stine*

Liberals

Liberals feel unworthy of their possessions. Conservatives feel they deserve everything they've stolen.

— *Mort Sahl*

You know it's easy to be politically correct and a liberal when you live in a gated community.

— *Bobcat Goldthwait*

Life

I think everyone just has to grow up a little and realize that, hey, life's rough for everybody. It sucks across the board. "Hi, I'm Bill, and I'm a birth survivor." I've got to live with that every day.

— *Bill Maher*

Life is a near-death experience.

— *George Carlin*

I was high on life, but eventually I built up a tolerance.

— *Arj Barker*

Life isn't like a box of chocolates, it's like a jar of jalapeños—you never know what's going to burn your ass.

— *Paul Rodriguez*

God knows life sucks. It's right there in the Bible. The book of Job is all about Job asking God to take away pain and misery. And God says, "I can't take away pain and misery because then no one would talk to me."

— *Bill Maher*

I remember when I was twenty-one. It's funny, because you think you know everything about life. But if you're twenty-one, I'll bet you can't name even one antidepressant. I'll spot you Prozac, whatever else you name I've got on me.

— *Ray Romano*

At first I thought that my life was going around in circles. Then I got to looking closer and it's actually a downward spiral.

— *Tom Ryan*

If life was fair, Elvis would be alive and all the impersonators would be dead.

— *Johnny Carson*

I understand life isn't fair, but why couldn't it just once be unfair in my favor?

— *Christy Murphy*

Who says life is sacred—God? Hey, if you read your history, God is one of the leading causes of death.

— *George Carlin*

Los Angeles

I have property in L.A.—a hotel is holding two of my suitcases.

— *Soupy Sales*

I'm from Boston and I moved to L.A. It's weird, it's crazy, it's different. Just meeting girls is different. Like in Boston, I meet a girl, "Wow! What a nice girl.

I hope my friends like her." Out here it's like, "Wow! What a nice girl. I hope she's really a girl."

— *Robbie Printz*

I moved to Los Angeles, and I miss so many things from the real world that they don't have here, like aging, pride, and dignity. People don't get older here, they just get tighter.

— *Greg Proops*

L.A. is a sick place to live. Earthquakes? People aren't scared. Riots? Hey, that happens. Cigarettes? Run for your life! Someone get me a pasta salad and a motivational cassette tape!

— *Richard Jeni*

How do people meet their neighbors out in L.A.? I'm from the South where we had block parties and cook-outs. In L.A. the only time my wife and I had a chance to socialize was at a local crime scene. It's so bad, now it's like, "Honey! Did you just hear that? Sounded like gunfire! Well, hurry up . . . put your nice clothes on. There are folks to meet!"

— *Bob Oshack*

I have some good news. We've been working very hard for this, and in 1999 Los Angeles will host the

Apocalypse. We got it. Let's all walk around a little prouder, shall we?

— *Patton Oswalt*

Lounge

It seems like a lotta people my age are into lounge culture. We still don't want to be our parents, but we'll dress like our grandparents. They represent a time of values, discipline, and jobs, but we'll settle for the pants.

— *Mike Maron*

Love

Love is a feeling you feel when you're about to feel a feeling you never felt before.

— *Flip Wilson*

I fall in love really quickly and this scares guys away. I'm like, "I'm in love with you, I want to marry you, I want to move in with you." And they're like, "Ma'am, give me the ten bucks for the pizza and I'll be outta here."

— *Penny Wiggins*

Lover

I'm a great lover—I bet.

— *Emo Philips*

I'm not a good lover, but at least I'm fast.

— *Drew Carey*

Luck

My lucky number is four billion, which usually doesn't come in handy when you're gambling. "Come on, four billion . . ."

— *Mitch Hedberg*

Magic

Fox had a show on, *Magic's Biggest Secrets Finally Revealed.* Did you see that? And I'm thinking the biggest secret I don't quite get—David Copperfield and Claudia Schiffer. How did he do that?

— *David Letterman*

Marriage

It's a little bit dangerous out there, and I guess men have to choose between marriage and death. I guess they figure that with marriage at least they get meals. But then they get married and find out we don't cook anymore.

— *Rita Rudner*

I have a Y chromosome that makes me ask, Why get married? But I wouldn't want to put down marriage as a whole—which it is.

— *Kevin Hench*

Being happily married is like having a shit job with people you dig.

— *Jack Coen*

They say married men live longer—it just seems longer.

— *Bobby Slayton*

The problem with marriage is that it involves men and women. And that's a pretty bad match.

— *Cathy Ladman*

Marriage is a rough thing because you've got to open yourself up, take somebody into your private areas, your little cavern that only you have been in so they can go, "This is a mess." "That's my emotions, honey." "Well, rearrange it, so it suits me."

— *Warren Hutcherson*

I'd like to get married again, but I'm afraid of that marital commitment—we're talking two, three years of my life.

— *Maura Kennedy*

I do everything my wife says, I'm on autopilot. Because that way when I say no, it's like thunder. And then she says, "What are you talking about, *no*?" And I say, "I'm sorry—I'm just playing a game: *Maybe I Have a Say.*"

— *Jeff Garlin*

Marriage is very difficult. Marriage is like a 5,000-piece jigsaw puzzle—all sky.

— *Cathy Ladman*

I married this really pretty young guy. He could not fuck to save his life. It cost me money to get laid badly.

— *Whoopi Goldberg*

Marriage is not a man's idea. A woman must have thought of it. Years ago some guy said, "Let me get this straight, honey. I can't sleep with anyone else for the rest of my life, and if things don't work out, you get to keep half my stuff? What a great idea."

— *Bobby Slayton*

Most of the women in my family married for money, but not a lot of money. You can't go to a reading of a will in my family without someone asking, "Who's gettin' the tools?"

— *Laura Kightlinger*

Another myth is that a woman must be married by a certain age or she'll never find stability. Hey, I've got news for you, ladies, looking to men for stability is like going to Crispin Glover for psychoanalysis.

— *Dennis Miller*

My cousin Sheila is forty-three—wants to get married. At every wedding she has to catch the bouquet. She goes to this bouquet-catching summer fantasy camp.

— *Richard Lewis*

Masculinity

A man's not a man until he can find his way to Sears blindfolded, and the Craftsman tool department makes his nipples rock hard.

— *Tim Allen*

Masturbation

Secretary of Education Jocelyn Elders resigned because of opposition to her plans to make masturbation a high school course. Damn, just when there's something I can finally teach. I could write the manual. It's a hands-on course. And it has a great final exam.

— *Robin Williams*

You know what my favorite TV show is? *Xena, Warrior Princess.* They should just call it the *Patton Oswalt Masturbation Hour.* Big moon-faced amazon with a stick, beating people up—what god did I please?

— *Patton Oswalt*

You know you have a masturbation problem when certain things won't get in your way, like the hiccups.

— *Zach Galifianakis*

If God had intended us not to masturbate he would've made our arms shorter.

— *George Carlin*

Meat

We were meant to eat meat, we have fangs in our mouth. Everything with fangs eats meat. When was the last time you saw a lion stalking rhubarb?

— *Harland Williams*

PETA, the People for the Ethical Treatment of Animals, are against eating meat. They say, "Don't eat anything that has a face." My standards are a little more relaxed. I won't eat anything that has a job.

— *Nosmo King*

Meditation

I took up meditation. I like to have an espresso first just to make it more challenging.

— *Betsy Salkind*

Men

I'm the white Anglo-Saxon male: I'm everybody's asshole. Black people think I'm physically deficient and oppressive, gay people think I'm latently homosexual and overly macho, women think I'm oafish and horny, and Asians think I'm lazy and stupid.

— *Dennis Miller*

Men are always calling me a strong woman. I hate when I hear that because it only means one thing . . . I have to be on top all night long!

— *Jennifer Fairbanks*

I hate that book *Men Are from Mars, Women Are from Venus,* because men aren't from Mars, men are from women. Men come out of women, so if they're screwed up, it's all our fault—stop trying to blame it on other planets.

— *Cathryn Michon*

I wish men would get more in touch with their feminine side, and become self-destructive.

— *Betsy Salkind*

Women love men with problems. We look at a troubled man the way an architect looks at a dilapidated building. "How can I renovate you?"

— *Vanessa Hollingshead*

I'm at a point where I want a man in my life—but not in my house. Just come in, attach the VCR, and get out.

— *Joy Behar*

It's rough being a man. See, men have to have money, have to try to look good, have to have the right job, the right prestige; women can be working in McDonald's—we'll still try to get your phone number.

— *Sinbad*

I was talking to a businessman, and I said, "Don't you think most men are little boys?" And he said, "I'm no little boy! I make $75,000 a year." And I said, "Well, the way I look at it, you just have bigger toys."

— *Jonathan Winters*

According to a study, men whose wives nag them live longer. In a related story, next week Frank Gifford turns eighty-six.

— *David Letterman*

Men only have two feelings—we're either hungry or horny. I tell my wife, if I don't have an erection, make me a sandwich.

— *Bobby Slayton*

I figure the only time I really need a man is about once a month, when it's time to flip my mattress.

— *Pamela Yager*

Men in L.A. are so needy. A guy pays for your liposuction, he thinks he owns you.

— *Maura Kennedy*

Women like older men. My problem is that I'm twenty-three. My future wife is now probably fourteen. She has braces and thinks that only Leonardo DiCaprio really understands her.

— *Peter Berkowitz*

It is a point of pride for the American male to keep the same size Jockey shorts for his entire life. And so you have a man with a brand-new forty-inch waist who is trying to get into size thirty-six Jockey shorts, a man who is now wearing a combination of supporter and tourniquet. Proud men have gone to the brink of gangrene to maintain the interior fashion of their youth.

— *Bill Cosby*

There is truth in what they say about the sexes. Men like cars, women like clothes. I also like cars because they take me to clothes.

— *Rita Rudner*

Guys are like dogs. They keep comin' back. Ladies are like cats. Yell at a cat one time, they're gone.

— *Lenny Bruce*

A woman will not pull underwear out of her butt in public. She'll walk funny till she gets to a bathroom. But your man, being what he is, will draw attention to it.

— *Sinbad*

Messages

In the seventies you could play a record backward and hear satanic messages. Since CDs, Satan's been stumped by technology; he's going to have to wait for some Japanese to go to hell and help him out.

— *Brad Stine*

Microwave

I saw a stupid ad for a microwave that cooks in ten seconds. Are there really people who say, "I've been home for ten seconds, where the hell is dinner?"

— *Jay Leno*

Midwest

People from Minnesota make fun of people from Wisconsin—that's like warring trailer parks.

— *Jackie Kashian*

Nebraska is proof that hell is full and the dead are walking the earth.

— *Lizz Winstead*

Military

I spent five years in the air force, and if it wasn't for sexual harassment no one would have talked to me at all. An officer accused me of being a lesbian. I would have denied it, but I was lying naked on top of her at the time.

— *Lynda Montgomery*

I joined the army because I was eighteen and bored with the tenth grade.

— *Robert Hawkins*

The stealth bomber replaced the B-1 bomber, which was supposed to avoid enemy radar by flying at treetop level. Unfortunately, trees are at treetop level.

— *Jack Mayberry*

We spend so much money on the military, yet we're slashing education budgets throughout the country. No wonder we've got smart bombs and stupid fucking children.

— *Jon Stewart*

Gays in the military? Please! I spent four honorable years in the air force, trouble free. Of course, I have to admit it could get hair-raising. I flew a helicopter, drove an ambulance, and ran the beauty shop.

— *Michael Greer*

Remember the whole controversy about whether or not women in the service should be in combat? Can women fight? Can women kill? Yeah, I think so. Just have the general come over here and say, "Hey, see the enemy over there? I just heard them talking. They say you look fat in your uniform."

— *Elayne Boosler*

Mimes

I'm walking to work this morning and I see one of those mime performers. So the mime is doing that famous mime routine where he's pretending to be trapped in a box. And he finishes up, and thank God he wasn't really trapped in a box. And I see on the sidewalk there he's got a little hat for money. So I went over and I pretended to put a dollar bill in his hat.

— *David Letterman*

Some things aren't funny. Beatings aren't funny. Stabbings aren't funny. Mimes aren't funny. But beating and stabbing a mime—why is that hilarious?

— *Dave Attell*

If you shoot a mime, should you use a silencer?

— *Steven Wright*

The saddest thing about me talking all the time is that I am a gifted mime. I could have had a brilliant career; I just couldn't shut up.

— *Paula Poundstone*

Minorities

They added up all the people in this country who consider themselves a minority and it added up to more than the population of the country.

— *Bill Maher*

Models

I'm not a model and that's okay with me. Because I don't want to look like a whippet or any other shaky dog.

— *Karen Kilgariff*

Money

You ever have somebody owe you money, and have the nerve to wear new clothes around you? Brand-new clothes, and they point them out, like "Hey, look what I just picked up?" Well, did you see my money while you were down there?

— *Chris Rock*

Whenever I see one of those ads where you get eight CDs for a penny, and then you have to pay another penny for the next CD, I immediately call up and demand to know why the last one is so expensive. Why does it cost eight times as much as the others?

— *Bil Dwyer*

I saw a commercial that said you can get a house with no money down. How in the hell can you do that? Kill the people who live in it?

— *Shang*

A fool and his money were lucky to get together in the first place.

— *Harry Anderson*

Conservatives say if you don't give the rich more money, they will lose their incentive to invest. As for the poor, they tell us they've lost all incentive because we've given them too much money.

— *George Carlin*

I'm always amazed how the poor can take so much of our money and still remain poor—what are they doing with it?

— *Greg Proops*

Monthlies, The

I've been sort of crabby lately. It's that time of the month again—the rent's due.

— *Margaret Smith*

Mother

Instead of saying hello, my mother gets on the phone and says, "Guess who died?"

— *Dom Irrera*

Before I became a mother I was such a free spirit. I used to say, "No man will ever dominate me." Now I have a six-year-old master.

— *Sully Diaz*

My mom is one of those really angry moms who gets mad at absolutely everything. Once when I was a little kid I accidentally knocked a Flintstones glass off the kitchen table. She said, "Well, dammit, we can't have nice things."

— *Paula Poundstone*

The cheapest thing my mother ever bought was the peanut butter with the jelly inside. Peanut butter with jelly in the same jar, how low can you go? That's like buying a shoe with a sock sewn inside.

— *Chris Rock*

My mother has the most amazing "gay-dar," which is the ability to spot a homosexual anytime and any place. Ironically, she can't pick her car out in a parking lot, and I laugh watching her walk up to the wrong car, not noticing, until she has her hand on the door handle and screams, "Wait a minute, I don't drive an ambulance!"

— *Scott Silverman*

My mother's house—the Sufferdome.

— *Richard Lewis*

My family is so dysfunctional that when I looked up the word "dysfunctional" in the dictionary there was a picture of my mother.

— *Paulara R. Hawkins*

My mother is so passive-aggressive. She says things to me like,"You just can't seem to do anything right, and that's what I really love about you."

— *Laura Silverman*

My mother is a typical Jewish mother. They sent her home from jury duty—she insisted *she* was guilty.

— *Cathy Ladman*

When my mother makes out her income tax return every year, under Occupation she writes in, "Eroding my daughter's self-esteem."

— *Robin Roberts*

My mother gained a little bit of weight because she quit smoking. That's all right, but it's hard to listen to her reasoning. It's hard to have your mom tell you that she has an oral fixation and always has to have something in her mouth.

— *David Spade*

My mother is one of those Jewish women who think that Jewish people are perfect. Like when they picked up David Berkowitz, the Son of Sam, I thought she was going to have a heart attack. She called me two days later and left a message. "He was adopted. Talk to you later."

— *Judy Gold*

Every time I did something bad, my mother would say, "How could you? After all the sacrifices I've made for you." And she did, once a week she would kill a chicken in front of my photograph.

— *Joan Rivers*

The way I feel, if the kids are still alive when my husband comes home from work, I've done my job.

— *Roseanne*

My mom, she wakes me at six in the morning and says, "The early bird catches the worm." If I want a worm, Mom, I'll drink a bottle of tequila.

— *Pam Stone*

My mom is real sweet. When I was a little kid she wanted to throw a surprise party for me, but she couldn't get any of my friends to come to it. I walked into the house alone and there was my mom with a candle inside a Twinkie. And she said, "Surprise Bob, and I don't want to bum you out, but I can't stay."

— *Bob Saget*

I get those maternal feelings, like when I'm lying on the couch and can't reach the remote. "Boy, a kid would be nice right now."

— *Kathleen Madigan*

I think I'd be a good mother—maybe a little over-protective. Like I'd never let the kid out—of my body.

— *Wendy Liebman*

My mother always says, "If I ever get senile, just put me in a home. I don't want to be a burden to you." And I say, "Mom, I would shoot you dead before I would do that."

— *Laura Silverman*

If you're looking for a way to piss your mother off, here's what I suggest. Next time you're driving with your mother, stop in front of the local strip joint. Put the car in park and say, "I'll be right back. I just have to run in and pick up my check."

— *Judy Gold*

My mom had a range of two emotions: She was either pissed or trying to get you to feel bad for her. As a kid, she told me how she learned to swim. She got in a boat and someone took her out in the middle of a lake and threw her into the water. I said, "Mom, they weren't trying to teach you to swim. And when they shot at you, they weren't trying to teach you to deflect bullets."

— *Paula Poundstone*

Motivation

If you ask me, this country could do with a little less motivation. The people who are causing all the trouble seem highly motivated to me. Serial killers, stock swindlers, drug dealers, Christian Republicans. I'm not sure that motivation is always a good thing. You show me a lazy prick lying in bed all day watching TV, and I'll show you a guy who's not causing any trouble.

— *George Carlin*

Movies

My boyfriend won't see anything he terms a "chick film." That's any film where the woman talks.

— *Maura Kennedy*

Do we really need the re-release of the movies *Dirty Dancing* and *Grease*? People who go to see these films are the same people who see the face of the Virgin Mary in a sticky bun.

— *Leslie Nesbitt*

So I go to the snack bar. I don't think it should be legal to call anything that costs $18.50 a snack. "Those Twizzlers look good, do you have financial aid?"

— *David Spade*

Murder

You're not gonna believe this. I saw a murder. I got there five minutes after it happened. Apparently, from what I saw, the body fell onto a chalk line exactly the same shape.

— *Howie Mandel*

The right to life movement killed a doctor. Let me use their own terminology against them: They aborted a child in the 200th trimester. People in the right to life movement should get a life before they tell other people what to do with theirs.

— *Dennis Miller*

Probably the toughest time in anyone's life is when you have to murder a loved one because they're the devil. Other than that, it's been a good day.

— *Emo Philips*

A lot of times when they catch a guy who killed twenty-seven people, they say, "He was a loner." Well, of course he was a loner; he killed everyone he came in contact with.

— *George Carlin*

Serial killers always say, "I heard voices." Why don't those voices ever say, "Go dancing" or "Bake a cake"?

— *Dexter Madison*

Museum

I went to a museum where they had all the heads and arms from the statues that are in all the other museums.

— *Steven Wright*

Music

The other day I was sitting around the house listening to an Alanis Morrisette CD, and the doorbell rang, so I slipped the gun out of my mouth.

— *Vernon Chatman*

I love the opera. You can't sleep at home like that.

— *Larry Miller*

I used to want to bc a country-western singer, but I took a test and I had too much self-esteem.

— *Brett Butler*

I don't like country music, but I don't mean to denigrate those who do. And for the people who like country music, denigrate means "put down."

— *Bob Newhart*

At the Grammy Awards, Keith Richards became the first performer ever to accept a posthumous award in person.

— *Jay Leno*

The Annual Grammy Awards were held in New York City, and once again Radio City Music Hall was crammed with a cross-section of musical artists representing every stage of addiction and denial.

— *Craig Kilborn*

I'm sitting at the opera, and I'm thinking, "Look how much work it takes to bore me."

— *Dave Attell*

I only know three REM songs, and guess what? I don't like two of them.

— *David Spade*

I don't know how real these rappers are keeping it from their $6 million homes in Beverly Hills, rapping about how rough it is. You write that in your Jacuzzi?

— *Warren Hutcherson*

I like hip-hop. I'm working with Ice Cube, Ice-T, and Herb Tea. I'm changing my name to Snapple.

— *Paul Mooney*

I've had it with Fleetwood Mac and their "revival" tour. I never thought I'd get sick of a band twice in one decade.

— *Dorothea Coelho*

Somebody asked me if I was going to see the Rolling Stones. If I want to watch an aging queen prance around to oldies for two hours, I'll rent a Richard Simmons video.

— *Bobcat Goldthwait*

I'm thirty-two and I'm in a band, but I go to covered-dish parties and I have ointment. That's just not rock and roll. I'm going on tour to rock the world, but I have to make sure I've packed my ointment.

— *Greg Behrendt*

It's been a long time since they've been on the road, but it was announced that Culture Club and Boy George will tour the United States. The tour will begin in Atlanta and probably end somewhere in a Beverly Hills rest room.

— *Bill Maher*

Musicals

Cats became the longest-running Broadway musical in history. And as a special treat, the cast was given tuna instead of dry food.

— *David Letterman*

Names

I don't remember names—I remember faces. You should be introduced by the face. Whatever it is you remember about that person. "Big Nose, Short Pants, come here a second. This is my friend, Hawaiian Shirt, Bad Haircut. Broken Glasses, Food-Stuck-in-His-Teeth." Whatever you remember.

— *Paul Reiser*

Neighborhood

I grew up in such a tough neighborhood, I remember laying in bed at night and looking up at the stars and thinking, like "Where the hell's the roof?"

— *Rocky LaPorte*

Neighbors

The guy who lives across the street from me has a circular driveway, and he can't get out.

— *Steven Wright*

New Age

I'm in favor of personal growth as long as it doesn't include malignant tumors.

— George Carlin

Ya think there are New Age kid's games, people? Fun games like Kick the Can to the Recycling Bin; Hide, and Then Find Yourself.

— Jackie Kashian

I have friends who are very New Agey. Always clutching their crystals: "My crystal help me, and protect me, and guide me . . ." Look, you live in your van. I don't think it's working for you. Maybe a shower would help, followed by work of some sort.

— Matt Weinhold

News

ABC News says Americans spend $300 billion every year on games of chance, and that doesn't include weddings and elections.

— Argus Hamilton

John Hinkley is the guy who shot President Reagan.
He recently asked the court for more freedom. He
says he wants twelve hours a month of unsupervised
time. Twelve hours a month to himself. Hey, even
married guys don't get that.

— *Jay Leno*

The assassin of Dr. Martin Luther King, James Earl
Ray, is dead. And what a practical joke on him when
he finds out that hell is integrated.

— *Bill Maher*

The Teamster's Union is broke. Things are so bad,
they may have to lay off 100 congressmen.

— *Jay Leno*

In an interview with the BBC, O.J. Simpson said that
he never talks to his children about their mother's
death. Although he is fond of telling the story of how
he lopped off Ron Goldman's head with a butcher
knife.

— *Colin Quinn*

Apparently, O.J. Simpson is taking correspondence
courses to become a lawyer. I think that's a great

idea. He's going to save so much money on his next murder.

— *David Letterman*

After a Los Angeles restaurant refused to seat him, O.J. Simpson demanded and got $500 in compensation. In addition, the restaurant must now also offer separate Murderer and Non-murderer sections.

— *Norm MacDonald*

You know what Teddy Kennedy said to O.J.? "Schmuck, you should have drowned her—the only thing you lose is your driver's license."

— *Soupy Sales*

Russia, not satisfied with poisoning the world with Chernobyl, has unveiled their plans for a fleet of floating nuclear power stations, the first one near Alaska. To ease concerns that a nuclear accident would destroy the Arctic people's life, Russian officials are telling Eskimos that having children with blowholes and fins will make fishing a snap.

— *Craig Kilborn*

Japanese Prime Minister Tomiichi Murayama apologized for Japan's part in World War II. However, he still hasn't mentioned anything about karaoke.

— *David Letterman*

Not too good a birthday for Saddam Hussein: Syria's present was chemical weapons. And you could tell by the look on his face when he opened it, he already has some.

— *Bill Maher*

China says it wants to start putting people in space. Not to explore, just to get rid of some of them.

— *Jay Leno*

Palestinians are throwing rocks at the Israelis. The Israelis are responding by blowing up their houses . . . which just gives them more rocks.

— *Jack Mayberry*

In their annual pilgrimage to Mecca, over 100 of the Muslim pilgrims died in the stampede while performing a ritual called Stoning the Devil. Unfortunately for them, the devil was performing a ritual known as Crushing the Pilgrims.

— *Colin Quinn*

Pol Pot, the dictator, and brutal mass murderer of Cambodia, was finally cremated. And he's going to hell, God decided, because hell was finally bad enough for Pol Pot once he would be condemned to a lifetime of listening to Milli Vanilli.

— Bill Maher

Boris Yeltsin cleaned out his entire cabinet recently. He got rid of the Jack Daniel's, the Beefeaters, the Wild Turkey.

— Leslie Nesbitt

New York

I had to move to New York for health reasons. I'm extremely paranoid and New York is the only place my fears are justified.

— Anita Wise

New York is like living inside Stephen King's brain during an aneurysm.

— Kevin Rooney

New York City is having some tough times; they're trying to save money. The New York City police department as a budgetary consideration switched over to one-size-fits-all body bags.

— *David Letterman*

New York—in the event of a nuclear attack, it'll look the same as it did before.

— *Billy Connolly*

I love being in New York, man. You don't know what you're going to see. I was walking around downtown today, I saw Angela Lansbury in an antique shop. For eight hundred bucks.

— *Jeffrey Ross*

Nosy

My wife thinks I'm too nosy. At least that's what she keeps scribbling in her diary.

— *Drake Sather*

Office

I used to work in an office. They're always so mean to the new girl in the office. "Oh, Caroline, you're new? You have lunch at nine-thirty."

— *Caroline Rhea*

Frankly, I don't believe people think of their office as a workplace anymore. They think of it as a stationery store with Danish. You want to get your pastry, your envelopes, your supplies, your toilet paper, six cups of coffee—and then you go home.

— *Jerry Seinfeld*

Pantyhose

I hate pantyhose. Although I occasionally wear Control Top because I've found there's no quicker way to flatten my tummy—and shut down my whole digestive tract.

— *Mercedes Wence*

Parents

Parenting is the easiest job to get—you just have to screw up once and it's yours. Thirteen-year-olds having babies so that they can feel grown-up—what happened to trying on Mom's heels and makeup? Christ, I still do that.

— *Dennis Miller*

There are no perfect parents. Even Jesus had a distant father and a domineering mother. I'd have trust issues, if my father allowed me to be crucified.

— *Bob Smith*

My father was a pimp and my mother was a prostitute. In my neighborhood "yo mama" games were very popular, but no one played them with me. What were they gonna say? "Lydia, yo mama's a ho." "Yeah, and she gets paid! But yo mama gives it away for free—that makes her a stupid, po' ho!"

— *Lydia Nicole*

My father's a proctologist. My mother is an abstract artist. That's how I view the world.

— *Sandra Bernhard*

If my parents lived with me now, I'd get even. I'd make them sleep in separate bedrooms. My mother would say, "What? Are you crazy? I've been sleeping with this man for years." I'd say, "Look, I don't care what you do on the outside. But when you're in my house . . ."

— *Elayne Boosler*

My parents have been married for fifty-five years. The secret to their longevity? "Outlasting your opponent."

— *Cathy Ladman*

My parents are willing to feed everyone in the world. They just want everyone to pick a date so they can defrost. Actually sometimes you don't want to eat their food. You want to cut out the middle man and throw that shit in the toilet. That's not true. What you really want to do is bury it.

— *Bob Saget*

Both my parents got high my entire life. We used to go on family trips together without even leaving home. I don't have childhood memories, I have flash-backs. I think that's why I hate to travel, because we never went anywhere. Oh wait, we did . . . rehab. That was fun.

— *Vanessa Hollingshead*

I could tell my parents were smoking pot when I was a kid. They'd go into their bedroom at eight, and we'd have smoke billowing from the ventilation system. The pot would go into the habit-trail where my hamster was running on its wheel, furiously. It would get a contact high, get off the wheel and lie down, and then it would eat everything in its cage.

— *Scott Silverman*

Peace

Whenever I hear about a "peace-keeping force," I wonder: If they're so interested in peace, why do they use force?

— *George Carlin*

Penises

I'm just a huge fan of the penis. Can I just say they're just the greatest? And they're all different—like snowflakes.

— *Margaret Cho*

My theory is that women don't suffer from penis envy. Every man just thinks his penis is enviable. Maybe Freud suffered from penis doubt.

— *Bob Smith*

Perfume

Why are women wearing perfume that smells like flowers when men don't like flowers? I've been wearing a great scent—it's called New Car Interior.

— *Rita Rudner*

Pets

Has any turtle ever outlived a shaker of turtle food?

— *Jerry Seinfeld*

I've always had pets. I know I should have a child someday, but I wonder, could I love something that doesn't crap in a box?

— *Sheila Wenz*

My goldfish got a bladder infection. I didn't know it was urinating thirty-seven times a day until its bowl tipped over, full.

— *Howie Mandel*

Philosophy

Albert Camus won the Nobel Prize for his novel *The Stranger,* which says, in effect, that life is meaningless. But that novel's dust jacket carried a paragraph reporting that Camus died in a car wreck in 1960. It should have added, "Not that it matters."

— *Dexter Madison*

Phobias

I suffer from peroxide-aphobia. Every time I've gotten near a blond woman, something of mine has disappeared. Jobs, boyfriends . . . once, an angora sweater just leaped right off my body.

— *Rita Rudner*

Piercing

I come from San Francisco. It's nice. There are a lot of people into body piercing. They get to where they look like they've been mugged by a staple gun. Fifteen earrings here, a little towel rack there.

— *Robin Williams*

I used to have an apartment in L.A. with roommates that had nose rings, and I couldn't concentrate on a word they were saying without staring at their nostrils. They could've told me the apartment just burned down and I'd say, "Uh, did that hurt going in? Can you pick your nose?"

— *Judy Gold*

How do you wake up one morning and say, "I'm going to get a steel rod shot right through the middle of my tongue. Then I'm going to get a steel rod shot through my cock. Then I'm getting a keychain attached to my balls, so I'll always know where my keys and my balls are."

— *Denis Leary*

A friend of mine got her clitoral hood pierced. I think that's disgusting. I would never do that, I'd get a clip-on.

— *Sarah Silverman*

I think men who have a pierced ear are better prepared for marriage. They've experienced pain, and bought jewelry.

— *Rita Rudner*

I don't understand the body piercing movement. I see some guy who's got eight rings through his eyebrows. I ran up and hung a shower curtain on his face. What about the people with the rings in their noses? Wouldn't it be great if you could walk up to those freaks, rip the rings out, and ten seconds later they'd blow up?

— *Harland Williams*

PMS

I thought I had PMS, but my doctor said, "I've got good news and bad news. The good news is, you don't have PMS. The bad news is, you're a bitch."

— *Rhonda Bates*

Poets

Are poets imaginative people? Yes, they imagine people like listening to their poems. Is there a lot of money in poetry? Yes. But first you must be completely dead.

— *Paul Alexander*

Police

Sometimes the police get carried away with those uniforms. I got a ticket for jaywalking and I was petrified. This policeman comes up to me. He has this great big helmet, big black boots, sunglasses, and the belt with all the stuff hanging off it. And he says, "Excuse me, little lady. Did you know you crossed against the light?" I had this terrible desire to say, "No, and do you know that you look like one of the Village People?"

— *Rita Rudner*

If you get pulled over, I think I've come up with the three most inappropriate things to say: "1. Hey, Quota Guy! 2. Wanna hit, dude? 3. Officer Bacon—I mean *Baker.*"

— *Jennifer Fairbanks*

Please, if you ever see me getting beaten up by the police, please put your video camera down and help me.

— *Bobcat Goldthwait*

I come from an Irish family in Brooklyn, a few stock-brokers, a smattering of intellectuals—and 40 percent of the New York police force. My uncle the cop used to read me bedtime stories: "Humpty Dumpty sat on the wall. Humpty Dumpty fell—or was pushed—from the wall. The perpetrator has not been appre-hended. Three male Hispanics were seen leaving the area."

— *Colin Quinn*

Politically Correct

I'm sick and tired of everybody worrying about being politically correct. It's all bullshit. For instance, there are no more car thieves. Now they're nontraditional commuters. Homeless people are full-time outdoors men. Prostitutes are sexual maintenance partners.

— *Paul Rodriguez*

They have a politically correct Bible now. They didn't want Jesus to be killed by Jews, an ethnic group, so he dies of secondhand smoke.

— *Bill Maher*

Politics

I looked up the word "politics" in the dictionary, and it's actually a combination of two words; "poli," which means many, and "tics," which means "bloodsuckers."

— *Jay Leno*

For some reason, people think it's an important measure of character whether our politicians have had affairs. But I don't think this comes within striking distance of our top thousand problems. If having sex with a politician could solve any of our problems, I'd volunteer to do it. And I don't even like sex.

— *Paula Poundstone*

The budget problems with Medicare and at NASA could be solved if the country began firing the elderly into space.

— *Al Franken*

The Department of Education is under fire for spending taxpayer money to close-caption the *Jerry Springer Show.* Oh, please, if you were watching *Jerry Springer,* can you read?

— *Jay Leno*

Presidential scholars say President Clinton's dog Buddy will be good for his image. According to these scholars, in comparison to a male dog, the president's sex life will seem relatively normal.

— *Norm MacDonald*

I think President Clinton misunderstood the role of the president, which is to screw the country as a whole, not individually.

— *Betsy Salkind*

According to a poll taken by *USA Today,* 38 percent of women said they thought Hillary Clinton would leave her husband after his term of office was over. The other 62 percent of women said that he'd promised them he would.

— *Colin Quinn*

The Clintons are a yuppie couple. She wants money for nothing, and he wants chicks for free. But I think he loves her, in his way. If not, why did he carve her initials into Al Gore?

— *Bill Maher*

Bill Clinton is like Kennedy Lite, with better driving skills.

— *Shang*

We've got six women in the Senate. Six women in the Senate? We are 52 percent of the population. Apparently women do suck at math.

— *Paula Poundstone*

The Senate decided they will be smoke-free. They ordained that all public areas in the Senate are now smoke-free. However, the senators themselves will still be allowed to blow smoke up each other's asses.

— *Bill Maher*

Newt Gingrich proposed a law against public breast-feeding. Yeah, he hates to see any kid get a free meal.

— *Billy Crystal*

In reverse order, our last eight presidents: A hillbilly with a permanent hard-on; an upper-class bureaucrat-twit; an actor-imbecile; a born-again Christian peanut farmer; an unelected college football lineman; a paranoid moral dwarf; a vulgar cowboy criminal; and a mediocre playboy sex fiend.

— *George Carlin*

The presidency is a young man's job. He rides herd on 180 million people. That's it—physical gig. Because, here's the parallel: You want to take a chance on a man over fifty-five when Mutual of Omaha won't? That's just for a policy—this is the presidency.

— *Lenny Bruce*

I'd never run for president. I've thought about it, and the only reason I'm not is that I'm scared no woman would come forward and say she had sex with me.

— *Garry Shandling*

Personal message to Pat Buchanan: Halloween's over, you can take the sheet off.

— *Billy Crystal*

They say we will never have a woman president of the United States because our hormones change once a month and it makes us crazy. Yeah, right. If a woman was president, she'd be like this: "Are you nuts? You take hostages on a day when I'm retaining water? I can't believe I have to sit here and waste my time with a morally bankrupt terrorist like you when there is a sale on and the stores close at six!"

— *Elayne Boosler*

Sonny Bono's funeral brought out a lot of political bigwigs. And Dan Quayle was there too. He was sitting in the back, thinking, "Well, it looks like I'm the stupidest politician alive, *again!*"

— *Nosmo King*

Have you ever wondered why Republicans are so interested in encouraging people to volunteer in their communities? It's because volunteers work for no pay. Republicans have been trying to get people to work for no pay for a long time.

— *George Carlin*

We have a presidential election coming up. And I think the big problem, of course, is someone will win.

— *Barry Crimmins*

Dan Quayle recently had his appendix removed. It's a useless organ that serves no particular purpose, but it seems a shame to break up a matched set.

— *Argus Hamilton*

Sadly, it's looking like Dan Quayle may run for president in the year 2000. My first clue is that he's starring on Broadway in *Grease,* as Rizzo.

— *Leslie Nesbitt*

Poor

My parents were very poor as I was growing up. I remember I wanted a dog one year, but they simply couldn't afford it. Nonetheless I persisted, so they finally broke down and got me a pet sponge. You laugh (I'm assuming), but it really wasn't all that disappointing. Sure, it couldn't sit or shake, oh, but momma could it *sop!*

— *Bob Oshack*

When I was a kid we were so poor that when my dad was in a car accident, we couldn't afford a steel plate for his head, so we had to use a paper plate.

— *Shang*

We were poor. If I wasn't a boy, I wouldn't have had nothing to play with.

— *Redd Foxx*

Pornography

Is it bad when you refer to all porno magazines as "dates"?

— *Patton Oswalt*

My husband says I don't understand pornography because I'm always fast-forwarding to the story.

— *Alicia Brandt*

My girlfriend hates porno, but we worked it out because we have two televisions. She's in the front room watching *Friends;* I'm in the back room watching *Really Close Naked Friends*.

— *Richard Jeni*

You know what I like more than women? Pornography. Because I can get pornography.

— *Patton Oswalt*

Post Office

The other day I went to the post office and I saw they had bulletproof glass. I realized that it wasn't to keep the bullets from coming in, but the other way around.

— *Louie Anderson*

Pregnant

When my best friend had her baby she gained eighty pounds. Oh, don't think I wasn't photographed next to her every day. I never looked thinner. She was in total denial. She asked, "Do you think there's any chance this baby could weigh up to eighty pounds?" "No," I said. "I'm your best friend and I'm going to have to go with forty-five tops. And I feel that's quite a chunky baby, really."

— *Caroline Rhea*

They caution pregnant women not to drink alcohol. It may harm the baby. I think that's ironic. If it wasn't for alcohol most women wouldn't be that way.

— *Rita Rudner*

Artificial insemination. That's a scary concept. You know why? I don't want to have coffee with a stranger, never mind have their child.

— *Rosie O'Donnell*

Psychic

Well, as I was driving, the phone rang. This was weird in itself, because the psychic had predicted that

I would get a phone call later in the day. As it turned out, it was my psychic calling.

— *Ellen DeGeneres*

I'm not going to apologize for this, but I have my own personal psychic. He doesn't predict the future, and he can't tell you much about your past. But he does a really fantastic job of describing the present. For instance, he can tell you exactly what you're wearing, but he can't do it over the phone.

— *George Carlin*

Racism

I think racism is a terrible thing. I think we should all learn to hate each other on an individual basis.

— *Cathy Ladman*

I mean, come on, jerks are everywhere, all colors, all races. All religions, too. Just look around you and take a moment to notice, and you'll see more ass-holes than a Turkish customs agent.

— *Dennis Miller*

Pretty soon racism will be a thing of the past. The ozone layer is going so fast, soon everyone will be black.

— *Shang*

I don't mean to trivialize racism, but if you can make a movie called *White Men Can't Jump*—why shouldn't you be able to make one called *Black People Can't Shut the Fuck Up in a Movie Theater*?

— *Bobby Slayton*

Traveling has made me a racism connoisseur. Ever been Down South? The racism there is just fucking perfect, stewed to perfection. Out in the open, everyone knows the deal, "Morning, nigger." "Morning, sir."

— *Dave Chapelle*

Reality

They say that one day through virtual reality a man will be able to simulate making love to any woman he wants to through his television set. You know, folks, the day an unemployed ironworker can lie in his Barca Lounger with a Foster's in one hand and a channel-flicker in the other and fuck Claudia Schiffer for $19.95, it's gonna make crack look like Sanka.

— *Dennis Miller*

Recycling

I have a friend who's so into recycling she'll only marry a man who's been married before.

— *Rita Rudner*

Redneck

Check your neck. You might be a redneck if . . .
You've ever lost a loved one to Kudzu.
You've ever used lard in bed.
There is a stuffed possum anywhere in your house.
Any of your kids were conceived in a carwash.
You've ever financed a tattoo.
You've ever worn a tube top to a wedding.
You have to go outside to get something out of the fridge.
Directions to your house include "turn off the main road."
You have an Elvis Jell-O mold.
In tough situations you ask yourself, "What

would Curly do?"
You bring your dog to work with you.
You watch *Little House on the Prairie* for
decorating tips.
You've ever hitchhiked naked.
You wife keeps a can of Vienna sausages in her
purse.
Motel 6 turns off the lights when they see you
coming.
You use a '55 Chevy as a guest house.

— *Jeff Foxworthy*

Relationships

I think I'm having low self-esteem about my relationship. I just failed one of those quizzes. One of the
questions was, "When is it okay to start walking
around naked in front of your new boyfriend?" I
answered, "When you want to end your relationship."

— *Caroline Rhea*

I can't get a relationship to last longer than it takes to
tape their albums.

— *Margaret Smith*

If you are married or living with someone, then there
is one thing that gets said day and night that drives

both of you absolutely crazy. But one or both of you always say it. It is "What?" The word, the phrase, the implication, the irritation. "What?" "You're deaf?" you mumble. "What?" "I don't mumble, stupid." "I heard that." "*That* you heard."

— *Elayne Boosler*

I should've known my last relationship was going bad. I was getting cranky. I said, "Will you keep the knitting down?" And sexually it was a nightmare. We got into bed and she said, "I'll race you to sleep." She wanted to save her orgasm for a rainy day. I called her breasts Mutt and Jeff. A couple of Amish friends came over for an erection raising. We were having problems.

— *Richard Lewis*

Some women go from one relationship to the next. Not me. It takes me forever to find a guy worse than the one I was just with.

— *Le Maire*

I'm not in a relationship now, but I have a stalker. Which is kind of nice, because at least he calls. And I never have to make plans with him, because he's always there for me.

— *Pamela Yager*

Religion

Every day people are straying away from the church, and going back to God.

— *Lenny Bruce*

Saw a guy with a sign that said, WHERE WILL YOU SPEND ETERNITY? Which freaked me out, because I was on my way to the Motor Vehicle Agency.

— *Arj Barker*

If you want to be a holy man, you have to be committed. When you make a decision you cannot waver in any way. You'd never see Gandhi during a hunger strike sneaking into the kitchen in the middle of the night. "Gandhi . . . what are you doing down there?" "I, um, I thought I heard a prowler . . . and was going to hit him over the head with this giant bowl of potato salad."

— *Jim Carrey*

It doesn't matter whether you're Republican or Democrat, liberal or conservative, Jewish, Catholic, Hindu, or Muslim. You trace it back—and we're all owned by Viacom, AT&T, or Time Warner. I recently read that Disney has actually merged with the Catholic Church. Apparently, the Vatican is now a theme park, and when the pope's in public he has to wear the ears. But aside from that, it's business as usual.

— *Mike Maron*

There's a religious group that goes door-to-door selling cosmetics. They call themselves the Jojoba's Witnesses.

— *Jeannie Dietz*

English is a spiritually challenged language: Why can't I understand a single word that a great spiritual leader like the Dalai Lama is saying, but I have to understand every syllable from Martha Stewart?

— *Beth Lapides*

Religion to me is like a sanitary napkin—if it fits, wear it.

— *Whoopi Goldberg*

The New Testament is not new anymore; it's thousands of years old. It's time to start calling it the Less Old Testament.

— *George Carlin*

The books of religion are beautiful works of fiction. These guys were great writers who wrote addendums to suit their fancies and made arbitrary rules. The important thing being that we keep the women in the backseat, that's the main gist of all religions.

— *Janeane Garofalo*

I'm Catholic and we don't read the Bible, we pay a priest to do that for us. Man's got all the week off and no wife, he can give us a forty-five-minute book report once a week. "Just weed through the crap and get to the plot, Padre."

— *Kathleen Madigan*

Even the Catholic Church is laying off priests and going to a new voicemail confession system. 1-800-FESS-UP. "Hello, you've reached the Catholic Church. If you're a bigamist, press 2 now. If you're worshipping Satan, press 666. If you've done something you're ashamed of with a farm animal, press BAA. Please do not touch your private parts as this will further delay your call."

— *Richard Jeni*

I grew up Catholic, but I hated nuns. When I was a little girl, I used to dress my Barbie in a nun's habit so she could beat the hell out of Skipper and not get in trouble for it.

— *Brynn Harris*

The Dodge-Plymouth dealers have just had their annual raffle, and they've given away a Catholic church.

— *Lenny Bruce*

Catholic churches have their priorities straight. Why feed the poor when you can always put up a new stained-glass window?

— *Brenda Pontiff*

Growing up Catholic in the '60s was magical. I was in awe of the Father, The Son, and The Holy Spirit— or as we called them, J.F.K., John John, and Ted Kennedy.

— *Brynn Harris*

There's only one difference between Catholics and Jews. Jews are born with guilt, and Catholics have to go to school to learn it.

— *Elayne Boosler*

If Jesus is my friend, why won't he lend me money?

— *Warren Hutcherson*

The Baptists are boycotting Disney because it wants to give health care to gays. That's ridiculous—I was checking my Bible and I found "Thou shalt not kill,"

"Thou shalt not steal." No "Thou shalt not give discount Tylenol to the Village People."

— *Richard Jeni*

I think what went wrong with Christianity is exactly like what happens when you try to get your dog to look at something on TV. Jesus pointed at God, and everybody just stared at his finger.

— *Frank Miles*

Why did Jesus die for my sins? I feel too guilty. Why couldn't He have just twisted an ankle for my sins?

— *Arthur Montmorency*

I belong to a Reform congregation—we're called Jews R Us.

— *Dennis Wolfberg*

The pope is a hard guy to please, isn't he? No weird sex. Well, what's this kiss my ring stuff?

— *Elayne Boosler*

I worry about the pope. You know he had a hip replacement. Now he has something in common with every little old lady on Miami Beach. Well . . . that and the hats and the dresses.

— *Bette Midler*

I was raised an atheist. Every Sunday, we went nowhere. We prayed for nothing. And all our prayers were answered.

— *Heidi Joyce*

Most people past college age are not atheists. Because you don't get any days off. And if you're an agnostic you don't know whether you get them off or not.

— *Mort Sahl*

I have as much authority as the pope, I just don't have as many people who believe it.

— *George Carlin*

I believe in reincarnation. I've had other lives. I know. I have clues. First of all, I'm exhausted.

— *Carol Siskind*

TV evangelists are the pro wrestlers of religion.

— *Rick Overton*

They say they don't favor any particular denomination, but I think we've all seen their eyes light up at tens and twenties.

— *Dennis Miller*

Every time I see a TV evangelist I can't help but think that if God wanted to talk to me through the TV, I think he could get a spot on a major network.

— *Margot Black*

In a swipe at President Clinton, Reverend Jerry Falwell noted that he's never been alone with any woman except his wife and daughter. Big deal. Woody Allen can say the same thing.

— *Jay Leno*

TV evangelists aren't holy men—they're just ambitious. I saw one guy who was so ambitious he actually became jealous of the Lord. You could tell halfway through his sermon when he said, "When I was a child, I wanted to be the savior of the world. Then they told me that Jesus was the son of God and I realized, it's all in who you know."

— *Jim Carrey*

Wouldn't it be great if we found you could only get AIDS from giving money to TV preachers?

— *Elayne Boosler*

Remote Control

I wanted one more remote control unit in my life. I want twelve of those suckers lined up on the coffee table—bring the friends over and go, "See those? I don't know how to work any of them. Zero for twelve."

— *Paul Reiser*

Right to Life

All of you who want to block clinics and deny the rights of others, here's what I propose: The Buddy System. Have it your way—all these kids need to be born, so now you get a buddy for eighteen to twenty-one years, federally assigned to you.

— *Janeane Garofalo*

I'd like the names of all the antiabortion people so that when all those kids start having babies, we can take them to their house.

— *Whoopi Goldberg*

I do, believe it or not, consider myself to be a Christian—and I'm sorry, but you just don't go shooting doctors. If a judgment's to be made, God gets to make it. Not you. Him. You are Barney Fife. Keep your bullet in your shirt pocket. All right?

— *Dennis Miller*

Rights

Everybody says they have rights. But you also have responsibilities. You have the right to choose any religion, but you also have the responsibility to pick one that doesn't wake me up on Sunday morning by knocking on my door.

— *Bill Maher*

Safety

For safety's sake, I try not to go to the ATM at night.
I also try not to go with my four-year-old, who
screams, "We've got money! We've got money!"

— *Paul Clay*

Men and women perceive crime differently. Once
when I was walking in New York with a boyfriend,
he said, "Gee, it's a beautiful night. Let's go down
by the river." "What? Are you nuts?" I asked. "It's
midnight! I'm wearing jewelry! I'm carrying
money! I have a vagina with me! Tomorrow," I
added, "I'll leave it in my other pants. Then we'll
go down."

— *Elayne Boosler*

School

Schools. I got an F one time on a question that asked my opinion.

— *Gallagher*

I'm not good at math—I've never been good at math. I accepted it from a very early age. My teacher would hand me a math test. I'd just write on it, "I'm going to marry someone who can do this."

— *Rita Rudner*

I was the total C student. If my son hands me his math homework, I'll have to say, "Hon, why don't you cheat off your little friends, or look it up in the back of the book like your father and I did."

— *Janeane Garofalo*

In school I was never the class clown, but more the class trapeze artist, as I was always being suspended.

— *Emo Philips*

And while we're at it, let's teach a follow-up class to sex education. Call it Reality 101—hammering home to a sixteen-year-old teen that he or she is going to have to quit school, quit video games, quit hanging out, and work a fifty-hour week dumping frozen chicken tenders into hot oil just so you can keep little Scooter Junior in Similac. Trust me, that's a bigger deterrent to teenage sex than the backseat of a Yugo.

— *Dennis Miller*

U.S. educators are reeling from the low math and science test scores of American students. We bombed in history, too. Over 90 percent of high school students think BC means Before Cable.

— *Argus Hamilton*

I remember reading how a bunch of high school kids were asked to define the Monroe Doctrine, and they thought it was a new band.

— *Whoopi Goldberg*

Intelligence tests are biased toward the literate.

— *George Carlin*

In high school, I was in the marching band, so you know the babes were all over me.

— *Drew Carey*

You know how to tell if the teacher is hung over?
Movie day.

— *Jay Mohr*

New York's Board of Education voted to require
school uniforms. The kids already have guns, might
as well give them uniforms too. The whole army
thing.

— *Jay Leno*

I remember my Catholic school days. It was awful,
being a Jew and all. They said,"You killed Christ, you
can't eat him, too." I had to bring my own Nilla
wafers.

— *Betsy Salkind*

Correspondence schools are full of shit. Saw an ad
where they claimed they could teach you veterinarian
medicine through the mail. Hate to be a dog in that
house. "Mail's here." "Yip, yip, yip." Talk about
being a regular in the pet store, "Hey, didn't I already
sell you a puppy?"

— *Drew Carey*

Don't go to your high school reunion. You know who
goes to your high school reunion? Idiots. Everybody
you hated in high school shows up. The really cool

people overdosed years ago, or they're living else-where under the witness protection program.

— *Billy Garan*

Your high school reunion. You get that letter in the mail. You feel like you only have six months to make something of yourself.

— *Drew Carey*

When I taught Sunday school I was really strict. I used to tell the kids, "If one more of you talks, you're all going to hell!"

— *Margaret Cho*

Science

Apparently a new galaxy is being formed or some-thing. But what it is, is they have discovered a huge cloud of dust there. And scientists believe if they could look and see under the dust, they would find an enormous exercise bicycle.

— *Bill Maher*

These two guys are now trying to clone human genes into cows, so that you'd get cows that would give human milk. Or maybe you'd get girls with four really big tits. I'm sure they think, "Either way, big improvement."

— *Cathryn Michon*

Self-Conscious

I was so self-conscious that when I was at a football game and the players went into a huddle—I thought they were talking about me.

— *Jackie Mason*

Self-Esteem

I have low self-esteem. When we were in bed together, I would fantasize that I was someone else.

— *Richard Lewis*

I think everyone has low self-esteem to some degree. Because no one can ever take a compliment. They either totally dismiss it or they confess some really horrible thing about themselves that you would never have otherwise known. You'll tell someone, "Oh, you have a beautiful smile." They'll say, "My back tooth is completely black." "Oh. Well. That's a beautiful dress you're wearing." "It was a dollar."

— *Caroline Rhea*

I find low self-esteem incomprehensible. Why hate yourself, when you can hate others?

— *Amy Ashton*

This guy told me he thought I was attractive, and when I get a nice compliment I like to take it in, swish it around in my brain . . . until it becomes an insult.

— *Sheila Wenz*

Separation Anxiety

Sometimes I have trouble getting out of the house at night. My wife and I are about to leave and my youngest daughter doesn't want to go to bed. She says, "Sleep with me. Sleep with me." She says it over and over again. It upsets me. I flash-forward twenty years and picture her saying it to the cable guy.

— *Bob Saget*

Sex

I once made love to a female clown, and she twisted my penis into a poodle.

— *Dan Whitney*

If you believe that there is a God, a God that made your body, and yet you think that you can do anything with that body that's dirty—then the fault lies with the manufacturer.

— *Lenny Bruce*

Just recently I was in bed with a woman, and, well, this will explain how screwed up I am. She said, "Don't you want to have an orgasm?" And I said, "What's in it for me?"

— *Richard Lewis*

I'm not good in bed. Hell, I'm not even good on the couch.

— *Drew Carey*

The other night I was making love to my wife, and she said "Deeper, deeper." So I started quoting Nietzsche to her.

— *Dennis Miller*

I'd like to talk about the sex I have with my wife, but when you're married you're not supposed to say, "Hey, I did my wife last night." It's okay if you're in a bar and say, "See that chick over there? I did her." People go, "All right. Good for you." But if it's your wife, they don't want to hear about it and you aren't supposed to talk about it.

— *Bob Saget*

My wife insists on turning off the lights when we make love. That doesn't bother me. It's the hiding that seems so cruel.

— *Jonathan Katz*

Sex after children slows down. Every three months now we have sex. Every time I have sex, the next day I pay my quarterly taxes. Unless it's oral sex— then I renew my driver's license.

— *Ray Romano*

I know my sexuality, but I get so confused by other people's. I don't even know the difference between transvestites and transsexuals. As I understand it, transvestites are the ones that grow down from the ceiling and transsexuals are the ones that grow up.

— *Pamela Yager*

I'm a quadrasexual. That means I'll do anything with anyone for a quarter.

— *Ed Bluestone*

I never believed in casual sex. I have always tried as hard as I could.

— *Garry Shandling*

No matter what she says or does, remember one thing—all women want it. But maybe not with *you*.

— *Bill Kalmenson*

I have so much cybersex, my baby's first words will be, "You've got mail."

— *Paulara R. Hawkins*

There exists a widespread folk myth that humans should learn about sex from their parents. My relationship with my father nearly ended when he tried to teach me how to drive. I can't imagine our relationship having survived his instructing me how to operate my penis.

— *Bob Smith*

When my teenage daughter told us that her sex-ed teacher had demonstrated how to put on a condom, my wife asked, "On what? A cucumber? Boy, are they letting you in for a big disappointment."

— *Robert Schimmel*

We need the Religious Right to take off their official Ralph Reed blinders and wake up. I know they'd rather have kids learn about sex the same way they did—from disgraced TV evangelists. But look, abstinence isn't working for priests these days, so I doubt it's going to work for teenagers cranked up on Nine Inch Nails and fruit coolers.

— *Dennis Miller*

When my daughter was growing up, I'd tell her sex was wonderful. Not too long ago I became a grandmother, so I guess she listened.

— *Whoopi Goldberg*

My three-year-old came in and saw me getting out of the shower. I was naked. She said, "Daddy, what's that?" She thinks it's a towel hook.

— *Bob Saget*

My problems all boil down to how I learned about sex. When I was little I asked my father, "What's a vagina?" He said, "It's an aerial view of geese." But then I asked, "What's a clitoris? Everyone's talking about it." My dad said, "It's a mouthwash." So I've spent the rest of my life looking for three women

who, by chance, happen to be walking in formation
while gargling.

— *Richard Lewis*

My mother was as religious as she was repressed.
Her facts-of-life speech began with the phrase, "Satan
takes many forms . . ."

— *Dana Gould*

I actually learned about sex watching neighborhood
dogs. And it was good. Go ahead and laugh. I think
the most important thing I learned was: never let go
of the girl's leg no matter how hard she tries to shake
you off.

— *Steve Martin*

In the year 2000, I think sex will be a lot different.
"Honey, I'm in the airlock now." "Okay, Bob. Leave
the sperm in the dish. I'll get it tomorrow."

— *Robin Williams*

Sex when you're married is like going to the 7-
Eleven—there's not much variety, but at three in the
morning, it's always there.

— *Carol Leifer*

I'm not an advocate of three-way sex. They're like that *Lucy* episode where Lucy and Ethel are trying to stuff all the chocolate into their mouths. I tried a five-way once, but I'm too needy. Afterward I was like, "So are we all in a relationship now?"

— Margaret Cho

My orgies are like the Special Olympics. Lots of drooling, but everybody's a winner.

— Matt Weinhold

When my wife has sex with me there's always a reason. One night she used me to time an egg.

— Rodney Dangerfield

If I ever wrote a sex manual, it would be called, *Ouch, You're on My Hair*.

— Richard Lewis

I'm at the in-between age. I still want sex very badly, I just want it before 10 P.M.

— Kim Castle

When a masochist brings someone home from a bar, does he say, "Excuse me a moment, I'm going to slip into something uncomfortable"?

— George Carlin

Women are really not that exacting. They only desire one thing in bed. Take off your socks. And by the way—they're not going to invite their best girlfriend over for a threesome, so you can stop asking.

— *Dennis Miller*

Making love to a woman is like baking a turkey: You have to preheat the oven, stuff, baste, make some gravy—put it in for two hours, take it out—not done yet. Another hour, another hour—finally it's ready. Men, it's microwave cooking. Rip off the package, three minutes, *Ding!* Gotta nap for an hour.

— *Craig Shoemaker*

The basic conflict between men and women sexually is that men are like firemen. To us, sex is an emergency, and no matter what we're doing we can be ready in two minutes. Women are like fire. They're very exciting, but the conditions have to be exactly right for it to occur.

— *Jerry Seinfeld*

Safe sex confused Hispanics. To us, safe sex is locking the doors.

— *Paul Rodriguez*

If I have phone sex to avoid getting pregnant, is that caller IUD?

— *Margot Black*

Safe sex is very important. That's why I'm never doing it on a plywood scaffolding again.

— *Jenny Jones*

Phone sex—I got an ear infection.

— *Richard Lewis*

I have so much phone sex that if I had a child it would be born with a dial tone.

— *Paulara R. Hawkins*

In an article in *Newsweek* I noticed the phrase "sexually illiterate." I didn't understand. Does anybody's penis read? Mine doesn't. It will look at pictures. But I have never seen it yawn and put a bookmark in.

— *Garry Shandling*

I'm scared of sex now. You have to be. You can get something terminal, like a kid.

— *Wendy Liebman*

Men in power always seem to get involved in sex scandals, but women don't even have a word for "male bimbo." Except maybe "Senator."

— *Elayne Boosler*

Monogamous sex isn't boring. It's like a really great book that you don't want to end—and then it doesn't.

— *Beth Lapides*

You can't stop kids from having sex—it feels good. And if it don't, get a new partner.

— *Whoopi Goldberg*

Shaving

I cut my Adam's apple shaving. What a mess . . . apple juice everywhere.

— *Drake Sather*

I bought a new razor. The one with the sensor. I saw it on the Super Bowl, where all the major shaving breakthroughs debut. It's double-bladed; the first one is psychic and the second blade is omnipotent. They make it sound like you have to lock it in a box at night or it'll shave you while you're asleep.

— *Jake Johannsen*

Shopping

Everything at IKEA requires assembly: I bought a pillow, and they gave me a duck.

— *Todd Glass*

My wife took me to the Price Club. I said, "Honey, we've got to get out of here—giants live here." Even the customers were huge. This lady in the aisle was so huge she had three skinny ladies orbiting around her.

— *Bobby Collins*

Why is it in America that buying something, just about any transaction you can name is as nerve-racking as a Bosnian grocery run? Why is it that seemingly everyone with a job along the great service highway is an uninterested sociopath with the interpersonal skills of a wolverine?

— *Dennis Miller*

I bought some batteries, but they weren't included, so I had to buy them again.

— *Steven Wright*

My new dress. Do you like it? It's from my favorite designer, On Sale.

— *Rita Rudner*

My wife will buy anything marked down. Last year she bought an escalator.

— *Henny Youngman*

Radio Shack's slogan is "You have questions, we have answers." Would it kill them to be honest with their slogan? For instance, "You have questions, we have a dumb guy who doesn't know shit about electronics. He can barely match his shirt with his tie and when you finally do buy something he's gonna ask you so many questions about your address and so forth that you'll want to punch him right in his stupid high-school dropout face."

— *Todd Glass*

You know you're never more indignant in life than when you're shopping in a store you feel is beneath you and one of the other customers mistakes you for one of the employees of that store.

— *Dennis Miller*

Shoes—that's a tough racket. I know, I buy shoes. Actually, I found a great pair of shoes today, but they only had them in size nine, so I lied to the guy.

— *Jonathan Katz*

My husband won't try anything on—not even shoes. He'll just hold the box up to the light and say, "Yeah, these fit."

— *Rita Rudner*

They've combined the all-night minimarket with the twenty-four-hour gas station to give you a one-stop robbery center. This way criminals don't have to drive around all night wasting gas. You shoot the attendant at 9:15, you're in bed by 11.

— *Jay Leno*

I went into a general store. They wouldn't let me buy anything specifically.

— *Steven Wright*

Shy

Science has found the gene for shyness. Yeah, they would've found it earlier, but it was hiding behind a couple other genes.

— *Jonathan Katz*

Sincerity

Sincerity is everything. If you fake that, you've got it made.

— *George Burns*

Single

You know, when you're in the grocery store at midnight, on a Friday night, buying fifteen dollars' worth of cat food, and you're a single woman in her mid-thirties . . . well, that's a special feeling.

— *Julia Sweeney*

I'm forty and single . . . Don't you think it's a generalization that you should be married at forty? That's like looking at somebody who's seventy and saying, "Hey, when are you gonna break your hip? All your friends are breaking their hips—what are you waiting for?"

— *Sue Kolinsky*

I love New Age jargon. You don't have to admit to being single. You can just say, "I'm learning to be there for myself on a daily basis."

— *Vanessa Hollingshead*

It's still fun being single. You just have to be more careful. You have to think about your own welfare. For instance, you can test people before you date them. Say, "Hi, ready in a second. I'm just sewing this button on my jacket." Then you have a little slip. "*Oops,* I just pricked your finger on this slide."

— *Elayne Boosler*

Sleep

I hate it when my foot falls asleep during the day because that means it's going to be up all night.

— *Steven Wright*

Sleep is death, without the responsibility.

— *Fran Liebowitz*

Right on the alarm clock is the snooze bar, which is basically a built-in cheating option. I don't know why I didn't think of it sooner, but finally I just taped it down.

— *Arj Barker*

I had this really bad nightmare in which I was in a restaurant and eating dinner and discussing the meaning of life with Steven Seagal and Kelly LeBrock, and they knew the answers.

— *Shashi Bhatia*

Smoking

They say if you smoke you knock off ten years. But it's the last ten. What do you miss? The drooling years?

— *John Mendoza*

It was different when we were kids. In second grade, a teacher came in and gave us all a lecture about not smoking, and then they sent us over to arts and crafts to make ashtrays for Mother's Day.

— *Paul Clay*

I have this one friend, Patty, who has smoked like four packs of cigarettes a day for something like twenty years. Now she has that deep, gravelly voice. It's so annoying and gross. Anyway, she visited me a few weeks ago. She kept rubbing her eye. "She finally said, "I got something in my eye. Look at it. What's in it?" "It's a fucking tumor, Patty," I said. "Quit smoking."

— *Judy Gold*

It's good to see people not smoking. You get dressed up, and you smoke, it gets in your clothes. You go, "What should I wear tonight, honey? How about something menthol?"

— *George Lopez*

Now cigar smoking is cool for women. I say, "God bless ya." Really. Whenever I'm in an intimate situation with a pretty gal, I want her to remind me as much as possible of Edward G. Robinson.

— *Richard Jeni*

They say that kissing a smoker is like licking an ash-tray—which is a good thing to remember the next time you get lonely.

— *Fred Stoller*

I just quit smoking. I took this course that tells me to breathe deeply every time I have an urge to smoke. Now I'm chain breathing; I paid 400 bucks to hyperventilate.

— *Craig Shoemaker*

I quit smoking. I feel better. I smell better. And it's safer to drink out of old beer cans laying around the house.

— *Roseanne*

You know what bugs me? People who smoke cigars in restaurants. That's why I always carry a water pistol filled with gasoline.

— *Paul Provenza*

I think we could end a lot of this intolerance in America if we all smoked cigarettes. You'd be hard-pressed to find a cigarette smoker who's prejudiced, because we smokers know something you nonsmokers don't—that we're all black on the inside.

— *John Hope*

The South

For a black man, there's no difference between the North and the South. In the South they don't mind how close I get so long as I don't get too big. In the North they don't mind how big I get so long as I don't get too close.

— *Dick Gregory*

I've found that the friendliest people are in the South. When I'm in New York in a hotel and check my messages, they say, "Is your light on? No." But in the South the answer is different. They say, "Yes, you do. Billy called. I think he likes you."

— *Caroline Rhea*

I was in Little Rock, Arkansas, and I noticed they didn't win at genetic roulette. And a lot of these people—can we talk?—got this eye that at an early age is looking down, the other one is revolving around their head. That scared me. I like to look at a man and a woman right in the eye, I don't wanna work for eyesight.

— *Bobby Collins*

In New Orleans: I don't know how they had slavery down here, it's so hot. Slaves would have quit, say "Fuck you—carry this shit yourself."

— *Richard Pryor*

Speech

This country was settled by people who did not want to be censored, who wanted the freedom to say what they felt. That's why they came here and killed the Indians in the first place.

— *Dennis Miller*

Sports

I like sports because I enjoy knowing that many of these macho athletes have to vomit before a big game. Any guy who would take a job where you gotta puke first is my kinda guy.

— *George Carlin*

I bought a newspaper the other day and I was gonna flip to the sports section when I realized I just don't want to read about vicious brawls, random drug testing, salary squabbles, or venomous court proceed-

ings. For chrissakes, it's enough to make you wanna
go to the front page.

— *Dennis Miller*

Mike Tyson hit this dude so hard I shit on myself,
and I was at home watching.

— *David Allen Grier*

I think it was Leo Durocher who said, "Baseball is
our national pastime." And I think it was Heidi Fleiss
who said, "Yeah, right."

— *Richard Jeni*

I'd like to see the Marv Alpert–Mike Tyson fight.
Tyson was a convicted rapist; he was still qualified to
box. Until he bites a guy. With that line of reasoning
he could have fucked Holyfield and they would have
kept the fight going.

— *Bobcat Goldthwait*

According to a new survey, 76 percent of men would
rather watch a football game than have sex. My question is, why do we have to choose? Why do you think
they invented halftime?

— *Jay Leno*

How come none of these boxers seem to have a losing record?

— *George Carlin*

Take boxing, the simplest, stupidest sport of all. It's almost as if these two guys are just desperate to compete with each other, but they couldn't think of a sport. So they said, "Why don't we just pound each other for forty-five minutes? Maybe someone will come watch that."

— *Jerry Seinfeld*

Certain sports are not ethnically conducive. I admire white people for coming up with bungee jumping. What kind of drug were you on when you came up with that? Where's the fun? If you ever see any Mexicans hanging upside down from a bridge with their feet tied, call the cops. Someone is trying to kill us.

— *Paul Rodriguez*

The NFL says it will punish any player who commits a crime, uses a weapon, or assaults a woman. "If a player feels compelled to engage in such behavior," the league says, "he can run for office like everybody else."

— *Argus Hamilton*

I think Foosball is a combination of soccer and shish kebabs. Foosball messed up my perception of soccer, I thought I had to kick the ball, then spin around and around.

— *Mitch Hedberg*

Playing golf the other day I broke seventy. That's a lot of clubs.

— *Henny Youngman*

Women are now referees for the NBA, and they're driving some guys crazy. They don't just call a foul, they want to talk about why it happened.

— *Leslie Nesbitt*

In Texas they passed a petition where girls can play high school football with the boys. I think if she's tough enough to play, she should play. If she's tough enough to play, she'd be hell that one week of the month. "I'm cranky, I'm bloated, my nipples hurt. Coach, gimme the ball!"

— *B.T.*

Who needs the NFL with all of their stupid rules like "no taunting"? You can hit a guy at full speed and put him in the hospital, but you can't say "Nah nah! Quarterback has a big butt!"

— *Drew Carey*

I've been watching the Classic Sports Network lately, and I must say, the Chicago Bears are looking good in 1985. Also, keep an eye out for a young coach named Vince Lombardi in the fifties—he's got something!

— *Bob Odenkirk*

My brother-in-law died. He was a karate expert, then joined the army. The first time he saluted, he killed himself.

— *Henny Youngman*

They had black people in the Olympics in the 1920s. Now, a brother was at the back of the bus in the sixties, then a brother must have been inside the engine of the bus, on a conveyor belt chasing a piece of chicken. Send my ass to the Olympics back then and America wouldn't have won a damn thing—I'd take the Javelin and throw it through the fucking judge's heart.

— *Chris Rock*

I was in Little League. I was on first base—I stole third. I ran straight across the diamond. Earlier in the week, I learned the shortest distance between two points is a straight line. I argued with the ump that second base was out of my way.

— *Steven Wright*

When Utah hosts the next Winter Olympics, things will be a bit more conservative. In the two-man Luge, they're gonna have a chaperone between the two guys.

— *Jay Leno*

Monica Seles is using this really huge racket. What kind of sport is tennis where you can change the size of the equipment because you suck at it? How does that work? Why don't baseball players just put on really long shoes, so they're always safe?

— *Dan Wilson*

Auto racing: slow minds and fast cars.

— *George Carlin*

On skiing: I pay approximately $1,300 for a lift ticket, which makes me eligible for the lift chair. I don't know who invented this death machine. This is like a psycho's physics test with benches whipping by. Suddenly you're inside a math word problem. Estimate the velocity of a bench . . . great, the one day I forgot my protractor.

— *Wayne Federman*

You'll never see two Vatos up on a mountaintop going "Check out the powder." If you see any blacks or Mexicans on top of a mountain, call 911. There's been a plane accident.

— *Paul Rodriguez*

I play tennis, and I'm pretty good, but no matter how much I practice I'll never be as good as a wall.

— *Mitch Hedberg*

You always know who's gonna win pro wrestling— the guy with the best nickname. Here from Philadelphia comes the iron man, Mike *The Hammer* Armstrong, and he will be wrestling . . . Eugene.

— *Dan Wilson*

Subway

I didn't find the New York subway scary, I thought
it was a little odd. Everywhere I looked were big
signs that said NO SPITTING. I don't know if I have a
big defiant streak in me or what, but I never even
thought about spitting till they brought it up. And
then it was all I felt like doing.

— *Paula Poundstone*

Superman

DC Comics is reviving Superman's old outfit. I
never understood Superman's clothes. We all got
used to the fact that he wears his underpants over
the leotard. But why do his underpants have a belt
on them?

— *Jay Leno*

The creator of Superman was Jerry Siegal. I'd never
thought of Superman as Jewish, but as it turns out,
he was using his X-ray vision to build up a dental
practice.

— *Bill Maher*

Surgery

I had surgery this year. Nothing serious, thank God. But just before I went under I heard the one thing you don't want to hear, "Where's my lucky scalpel?"

— *Jonathan Katz*

You know what type of cosmetic surgery you never hear about? Nose enlargement.

— *George Carlin*

My sister got some of the fat sucked out of her bum and injected in her face, so she'd have a much fuller face. Bad news is she doesn't look any better. The good news is I now officially get to call her ass face.

— *Harland Williams*

I don't have anything against facelifts, but I think it's time to stop when you look permanently frightened.

— *Susan Norfleet*

Survival

When you pick something up with your toes and transfer it to your hand, don't you feel, just briefly,

like a superior creature? Like you could probably survive alone in a forest for a long time? Just briefly.

— *George Carlin*

Stereotype

Some stereotypes aren't negative. You think African-
American males get mad that we make jokes they
have the biggest penises? Hell, no man, I'd switch
places in a second. I'm hung like a Tic-Tac.

— *Jeffrey Ross*

If you're Mexican and an actor in Hollywood, you
get to play all the "un-people"—undocumented,
unemployed, uneducated, on drugs.

— *Dyana Ortelli*

White people's stereotypical portrayal of Indians in
the movies used to get to me when I was a kid. I was
shocked when Chuck Connors was cast as Geronimo.
That's like hiring John Ritter to play Malcolm X.

— *Charlie Hill*

I have a bit of an identity problem. I'm like the only
Mexican who hasn't won the California lottery yet.

— *Paul Rodriguez*

Jesus is always played by a guy who looks like Ted Nugent. They never have a Jesus who is Jewish going, "I'm with lepers here, you bastards. I walked across the water. Give me a drink. Open the door."

— *Robin Williams*

Strip Clubs

I love the naked women when I know them and they're with me. But at strip clubs I pay a $10 cover, a beautiful nude woman dances inches away from my face, I can't touch her, she can't touch me, I can't touch myself, and I give her all my money. You know that's what hell has to be like.

— *Jeff Garlin*

Talk

How come when you want to talk to somebody, we ask them out to dinner—and busy the only orifice that we was interested in?

— *Gallagher*

Tattoo

A friend of mine had his girlfriend's name tattooed on his arm. Now, I can see marrying a girl and having a few kids. But a tattoo . . . it's so permanent.

— *Drake Sather*

I want to get a tattoo over my whole body—but taller.

— *Steven Wright*

Couples who get tattooed are the most optimistic people in the world about relationships. I don't want a former lover's name in my phone book, much less his picture on my ass.

— *Carol Siskind*

Telephone

The technological advance I wish I could get is an addition for my answering machine, a Get-to-the-Point button.

— *Alicia Brandt*

Neither of my parents understand how an answering machine works. When my mother leaves me a message she's actually trapped inside the machine. It is just like a desperate cry. "Carol? Carol? Carol? Are you there? Carol? I'm in the machine." And my father's even worse. He leaves me these messages, "Uh, tell her that her father called."

— *Caroline Rhea*

How does that phone cord get so tangled? All I do is talk, and hang up. I don't pick it up and do a cartwheel and a somersault.

— *Larry Miller*

I'm worried about all these 900 numbers that come on the cable channels. My daughter is very smart. I'm worried that when she gets a little older I'm going to get a phone bill and ask, "Honey, did you make these 900 calls?" And she'll say, "Yes, Daddy. I've been bad. Spank me, Daddy. Spank me real hard. Spank me good, Daddy." "Where'd you learn that?" I'll ask. "Which number was that? I just want to know so I can call it myself."

— *Bob Saget*

I hate my voice because I don't think it's sexy. I got an obscene phone call, and I actually felt guilty because I thought I turned the guy off.

— *Cathy Ladman*

I hated my boss so much I used to make prank calls to her house. I would wait for her eight-year-old daughter to answer the phone and I would tell her, "Barney's dead."

— *Paulara R. Hawkins*

It kills me the way they advertise phone sex, "Phone up and hear a woman's secret fantasies." If there's any reality to this, you'd hear stuff like, "Yeah, I'd like to be paid the same as a man for the same job."

— *Mike MacDonald*

There are 25,000 sex phone lines for men in the United States but only 3 for women. Apparently, when we want somebody to talk dirty and nasty to us we just go to work.

— *Felicia Michaels*

Television

As long as I have a cool TV, I might as well live in a cave. In fact, I like to think of my house as nothing more than a glorified console for my television—the ultimate stereo cabinet.

— *Drew Carey*

They have an amazing proliferation of TV channels now: The all-cartoon channel, the twenty-four-hour–science fiction channel. Of course, to make room for these on the dial they got rid of the Literacy Channel and What's Left of Fucking Civilization Channel.

— *Dennis Miller*

The best comedy show on TV: *Cops*. What's funnier than white trash under pressure? Nothing. And if TV was invented to make you feel better about yourself, then what's better than red-necked failure for thirty minutes?

— *Patton Oswalt*

I wish there was a knob on the TV so you could turn up the intelligence. They got one marked "brightness," but it doesn't work, does it?

— *Gallagher*

I'm pissed off. To this day, the only Latinos on TV consistently were the Menendez brothers. What is this? We've got to shoot our parents before we get on the television set?

— *Paul Rodriguez*

UPN is reviving *The Love Boat*. It says the new version is more realistic. This means whenever the cast asks for a raise, the captain runs the ship into an iceberg.

— *Argus Hamilton*

What exactly is viewer discretion? If viewers had discretion, most television shows would not be on the air.

— *George Carlin*

Why would anyone want to read *Soap Opera Digest*? You're reading gossip about people who don't exist!

— *Margot Black*

The final episode of *Seinfeld,* what a shocking end to the series. Honest to God, here's what happened: Jerry finally locked his door.

— *David Letterman*

The producers of *The Jerry Springer Show* said they're taking steps to keep their guests from hurting each other. In fact, they had an entire new set designed by Nerf.

— *Conan O'Brien*

Temperature

It doesn't matter what temperature a room is. It's always room temperature, right?

— *Steven Wright*

Therapy

Therapy is like a really easy game show where the answer to every question is: "My mom?"

— *Robin Greenspan*

I view a visit to the therapist in much the same way I view a visit to the hairdresser. When I leave the office my head looks great. But around an hour later it's all fucked up and I can't get it to look that way again on my own. Excuse me, doc, can I get a little mousse for my id?

— *Dennis Miller*

You know you're messed up when the therapist says, "*Really?* You freaky, ain't you?"

— *Sinbad*

I went to a therapist and he said to treat every day
like it's your last. So I did—I stiffed him.

— *Bob Zany*

Psychiatrists are no help. What do they tell you?
"Well, we'll have to get back into your childhood to
find the trauma." Who can't find the trauma in childhood? I'm two feet tall. I don't know what the fuck is
going on. Everybody can beat me up. Gee, doc,
you're a genius to find trauma there.

— *Bill Maher*

I had to get rid of my therapist; she wasted a lot of
time talking. And I asked, "Excuse me, but can we go
directly to the medication?"

— *Maura Kennedy*

My last shrink just retired. I'm freaked out about it.
She was only twenty-four. I guess I burned her out.

— *Richard Lewis*

A man goes to a psychiatrist. The doctor says, "You're
crazy." The man says, "I want a second opinion!"
"Okay, you're ugly too!"

— *Henny Youngman*

I told my mother that I was thinking about seeing a therapist. She thought that was a good idea because she heard they made a lot of money.

— *Darlene Hunt*

Time

Clinton is very upset about Daylight Saving Time because he loses an hour of sex.

— *Bill Maher*

No matter how much time you save, at the end of your life, there's no extra time saved up. You'll be going, "What do you mean there's no time? I had a microwave oven, Velcro sneakers, a clip-on tie." Because when you waste time in life, they subtract it. Like if you saw all the *Rocky* movies, they deduct that.

— *Jerry Seinfeld*

Do you remember to change your clocks? I think you Spring ahead, and you Fall back. It's just like Robert Downey Jr. trying to get out of bed.

— *David Letterman*

My parents live in the Central time zone. I talk to my father once a week, but he still doesn't understand time zones. "Well, it's 8 o'clock here, so what is it, 6 o'clock there, huh, huh? It's summer here, so what is it, winter there? It's the Industrial Revolution here, so is it the Paleolithic era there?"

— *Hugh Fink*

My watch is three hours fast and I can't fix it, so I'm gonna move to New York.

— *Steven Wright*

Time magazine celebrated seventy-five years of being the magazine you read in your dentist's office, right after you finish the word jumble in *Highlights*.

— *Craig Kilborn*

Why are our days numbered, and not, say, lettered?

— *Woody Allen*

The Times

The nineties are so Dickensian, "The best of times, the worst of times"—only without that "best of times" part.

— *Beth Lapides*

Titanic

The last telegram sent from the *Titanic* was recently auctioned off. It said, "Help—they won't stop playing Celine Dion's *Titanic* song." And then everyone killed themselves.

— *Conan O'Brien*

Tobacco Industry

The tobacco industry is under great duress. The creator of Joe Camel testified at a trial, said that he thought it wasn't there to encourage teens to smoke. However, it did make teenage boys put sunglasses on their penis.

— *Bill Maher*

Train

I don't trust trains. I remember those old movies where halfway through the journey somebody would reach up above the window and yank down on the brake cord. I don't want to be on any form of mass transit where the general public has access to fucking brakes. I'd hate to find out that we went off the tracks

at 200 miles per hour because Gus thought he saw a
woodchuck.

— *Dennis Miller*

Trauma

I'm suffering from post-post-traumatic syndrome, and
I'm going to keep talking about it until some cute guy
holds me.

— *Kathy Griffin*

UFO

Only man is narcissistic enough to think that a highly
evolved alien life force would travel across billions
and billions of light years in spacecrafts without windows, and then upon landing on our planet, that their
first impulse is to get into some hick's ass with a
flashlight.

— *Dennis Miller*

When I was in the middle of the desert a UFO
landed. Three one-inch-tall guys got out. They
walked over to me. I said, "Are you really one inch
tall?" They said, "No, we're really very far away."

— *Steven Wright*

Vacation

We took a cruise. It depends on the boat. You have to get on a good boat. They have the *Fantasy,* the *Ecstasy* . . . we were on the *Hysterectomy.*

— *Rita Rudner*

Babies don't need a vacation. But I still see them at the beach. It pisses me off. When no one's looking I'll go over to a baby and ask, "What are you doing here? You haven't worked a day in your life."

— *Steven Wright*

Vegetarian

My friend Larry says to me, "You should be a vegetarian like me, you'll be a lot healthier and live longer." So I pick up the steak, I flap it at him, and say, "This cow used to be vegetarian, and he's not looking that healthy to me. So you just watch your mouth, salad bar–breath, because when all the cows are gone we're coming hunting after you, lettuce eater."

— *Harland Williams*

Victoria's Secret

I was thrown out of Victoria's Secret—I gave the secret away, and they just frown on that.

— *Paula Poundstone*

Video

I've been watching so many videos, last night I had a dream with credits.

— *Lynda Montgomery*

I was watching this two-hour Hanson video the other day, and it turned out to be *Children of the Corn*.

— *Patton Oswalt*

Virgin

I used to be a virgin, but I gave it up—there was no money in it.

— *Marsha Warfield*

Voting

I know we don't like to vote—marking your ballot nowadays is like choosing between the 3 A.M. showing of *Beastmaster* on Showtime and the 3 A.M. showing of *Beastmaster 2* on Cinemax.

— *Dennis Miller*

Why does voting in a presidential election seem, at least to me, a lot like going into an adult novelty store and wondering which is going to be the least painful dildo?

— *Bobcat Goldthwait*

WxYz

War

It seems as if every year or so there's another new war breaking out somewhere. There was war in Sri Lanka. War in Beruit. War in Yugoslavia. In Croatia. Sometimes I think war is God's way of teaching us geography. Before the war in the Middle East, I didn't know what the hell a Kuwait was. I thought it was a fruit from New Zealand.

— *Paul Rodriguez*

I think we should attack Russia now. They'd never expect it.

— *George Carlin*

Washington

George Washington had fifty-five children with slaves, so he was also the illegitimate father of the country. We should take Washington off the dollar and put him on food stamps.

— *The Mooney Twins*

Wedding

On my wedding night I should have known better than to wear a nightgown with feet.

— *Joan Rivers*

I asked my wife, "Where do you want to go for our anniversary?" She said, "Somewhere I have never been!" I told her, "How about the kitchen?"

— *Henny Youngman*

Caucasians do things differently at their weddings than Mexicans do. Like, they send out invitations. Ahead of time. See, we pull up to the corner, "Hey Chuy! My cousin Carlos is getting married. Follow me!"

— *Debi Gutierrez*

I can't understand why I should give cut crystal serving trays as wedding gifts to guys who I knew only yesterday as Snot Boy.

— *Paul Provenza*

When we got married we registered at Blooming-
dale's because you can return everything for cash.
And I figure each place setting can keep me in beer
money for three months.

— *Gary Barkin*

Weight

You reach a certain age and your body doesn't react
like it used to. Fat just jumps on your body. When
you're in your twenties, you can eat a whole bag of
Oreo cookies. Nothing happens. I'm now in my late
thirties. I eat just one and my butt expands while I'm
chewing.

— *Sinbad*

It's hard to be famous and struggle with a weight
problem. I was in Baskin-Robbins—just looking—
and this lady said to me, "Are you Rosie
O'Donnell?" I said, "Yes." "I didn't know you were
pregnant." I looked at her and said, "Yes, four and a
half months." She kept asking, "What are you going
to name it?" "I don't know, either Ben or Jerry, I'm
not sure."

— *Rosie O'Donnell*

When I was young, I was fat. I was a fat little kid. But after careful research and calculation, I came to the inevitable conclusion that, hey, I'm eating too much.

— *Richard Jeni*

You know you're getting fat when you can pinch an inch on your forehead.

— *John Mendoza*

Weights

At my gym they have free weights, so I took them.

— **Steve Smith**

Wife

My wife finally convinced me to sign what's called a living will. It's a document that gives her the right, if I become attached to some mechanical device, to terminate my life. So yesterday, I'm on the exercise bike . . .

— *Jonathan Katz*

To please my wife I got in touch with my feminine side. Now I've got yeast infection.

— *Bob Zany*

Take my wife . . . please.

— *Henny Youngman*

Wigs

My wife is a natural woman, she don't wear wigs or anything. I don't really like women who wear wigs because it makes your head smell like a foot.

— *David Allen Grier*

Wine

I've been making wine at home, but I'm making it out of raisins so it will be aged automatically.

— *Steven Wright*

I read recently that wine can actually improve your health by reducing the risk of heart attack, hardening of the arteries, and cholesterol. This is good news, unless you're a wino. They see this, "Oh no, I'm getting better. That means eight extra years of sleeping in doorways wearing seven hats."

— *Jerry Seinfeld*

Women

Some say it's what's on the inside that count. If that were true about women, *Playboy* would be running centerfolds of brain tissues and gall bladders.

— *Christy Murphy*

On her wedding day, a Masai tribeswoman symbolizes her low status by putting dung on her head. American women may have to put up with a lot of bullshit, but at least we don't have to wear it.

— *Jackie Wollner*

Women don't need conventional tools, we'll use anything that's handy. But when pounding a nail, don't use a shoe—shoes cost $40 a pair. A package of frozen hamburger costs $2. Use the hamburger.

— *Jeannie Dietz*

All women want from men is a partner who will share his hopes, his thoughts, his dreams. And if you don't, we're going to bitch at you until the day you die.

— *Stephanie Hodge*

Work

I used to work at the International House of Pancakes. People complained all the time about the service. We weren't slow, the floors were sticky. We were stuck in the back trying to get to the tables.

— *Paula Poundstone*

Most people work just hard enough not to get fired and get paid just enough money not to quit.

— *George Carlin*

I called a temp agency looking for work and they asked if I had any phone skills. I said, "I called you, didn't I?"

— *Zach Galifianakis*

I worked as a receptionist, but I couldn't get the hang of it. I kept on answering the phone by saying, "Hello, can you help me?"

— *Caroline Rhea*

I work for myself, which is fun. Except for when I call in sick, I know I'm lying.

— *Rita Rudner*

The trouble with being in the rat race is that even if you win, you're still a rat.

— *Lily Tomlin*

Collaborative, from the Greek *col:* with other people; *laborative:* the other people are morons.

— *Richard Jeni*

To have some grins, I recommend going to a store and pretending you're an employee. When someone asks, "Do you work here?" tell them the televisions are free today.

— *Bob Dubac*

World

There are only two places in the world: over here, and over there.

— *George Carlin*

I once wanted to save the world—now I just want to leave the room with some dignity.

— *Lotus Weinstock*

It's a small world, but I wouldn't want to paint it.

— *Steven Wright*

Bios

Mark Alexander has appeared on innumerable TV shows, including *Evening at the Improv* and *Comic Strip Live.*

Paul Alexander has appeared on Comedy Central's *Comedy Product* and HBO's *Mr. Show.*

Tim Allen is the star of ABC's *Home Improvement,* and star voice in Disney's *Toy Story.*

Woody Allen is an Academy Award–winning director, writer, and actor of films that include *Annie Hall* and *Mighty Aphrodite.*

Larry Amoros has appeared on HBO's "Young Comedians Special."

Harry Anderson was the star of *Dave's World* and *Night Court.*

Louie Anderson is the host of NBC's *Comedy Showcase,* and has appeared and starred in a number of HBO comedy specials, including "Comic Relief."

Craig Anton was featured on the sitcom *First Time Out.*

Tom Arnold is an actor who has appeared in the films *True Lies, Nine Months,* and several sitcoms, including the eponymous *Tom.*

Amy Ashton was a model turned actress who then turned comedian when she grew tired of being stereotyped as either a bimbo or a bitch.

Dave Attell was nominated for an American Comedy Award for Funniest Male Standup Comic, and was featured in the HBO special "Mr. Vegas."

Joy Auerbach has performed on PBS's *Mark Allen Show,* the *Keenan Ivory Wayans Show,* and at the Comedy Store in Hollywood.

b

Bill Bauer is a comedian and sitcom writer.

Willie Barcena has appeared several times on *The Tonight Show.*

Arj Barker appeared on Comedy Central's *Comedy Product* and *Comics Come Home.*

Gary Barkin, an ex-lawyer, is now a voice-over performer and has performed at the Ice House and the Comedy & Magic Club.

Fred Belford belongs to the L.A. ComedySportz troupe.

Joy Behar is a comedian and actress who is now on the panel of the ABC daytime talk show *The View.*

Greg Behrendt has appeared on an assortment of cable comedy shows, from A&E's *Evening at the Improv* to *Caroline's Comedy Hour.*

Sandra Bernhard was a costar of *Roseanne* and has starred in a number of films, from *The King of Comedy* to *Plump Fiction.*

Shashi Bhatia has been featured on Comedy Central's *Stand Up, Stand Up* and in the movie *Leaving Las Vegas.*

Margot Black has appeared on Lifetime's *Girls Night Out* and *The Jenny McCarthy Show.*

Chris Bliss has gone from juggler to political comedian and become a regular on *The Tonight Show.*

Ed Bluestone was a seventies comic, now a book author, also known for having created *National Lampoon*'s best-selling cover ever: "Buy This Magazine or We'll Shoot This Dog."

Elayne Boosler has starred in her own HBO and Showtime specials, including "Party of One."

Mel Brooks is a comedian, writer, and director of such films as *Young Frankenstein* and *Blazing Saddles.*

Kathy Buckley is a motivational speaker and winner of a 1998 American Comedy Award.

Mike Bullard has appeared at the Just For Laughs festival in Montreal and hosts the Canadian talk show *Open Mike.*

Andy Bumatai is Hawaii's favorite comedian.

George Burns was a classic comedian whose career stretched from vaudeville to the *Burns and Allen* sitcom, and to the movie *Oh, God.*

Brett Butler was the star of ABC's *Grace Under Fire.*

Alicia Brandt is a standup comedian and an actress who has appeared in a range of roles from *General Hospital* to *Mousehunt.*

B.T. has performed on HBO's "U.S. Comedy Arts Festival."

C

Blaine Capatch is a writer/performer on *MAD TV* and has been featured on Comedy Central's *Comedy Product.*

Drew Carey is the star—coincidence or what?—of *The Drew Carey Show* on ABC.

George Carlin has won a Grammy, was nominated for an Emmy, and won a CableAce Award for his comedy albums and HBO and network comedy specials.

Jim Carrey is the star of the movies *Dumb and Dumber,* the two *Ace Venturas,* and *The Truman Show.*

Johnny Carson hosted NBC's *The Tonight Show* for more than thirty years.

Kim Castle is a comedian and an actress who has appeared in the movies *Freejack* and *Manhunter.*

Jeff Cesario has won an Emmy for writing *The Dennis Miller Show,* and has appeared on *The Tonight Show.*

In addition to starring in his very own HBO *Comedy Half Hour,* **Dave Chapelle** was the star and cowriter of the feature film *Half Baked.*

Vernon Chatman has appeared on *Late Night with Conan O'Brien,* Comedy Central's *Comics Come Home,* and *Full Frontal Comedy* on Showtime.

Margaret Cho has starred in her own HBO special and on the former ABC sitcom *All American Girl.*

Paul Clay is a sitcom writer.

Ellen Cleghorne was a featured player on *Saturday Night Live,* and of course, her own WBN series, *Cleghorne.*

Dorothea Coelho has proved that comedy can travel, having performed from Harrah's in Las Vegas to Reykjavik, Iceland.

Jack Coen has made ten appearances on *The Tonight Show* and no fools they, they made him a staff writer. He was also a contributing writer on HBO's *Larry Sanders Show.*

Bobby Collins was the host of VH-1's *Comedy Spotlight.*

Billy Connolly is a Scottish comedian who also recently starred in the Oscar-nominated film, *Her Majesty Mrs. Brown.*

Bill Cosby has starred in a number of TV shows, from *I Spy* to *The Cosby Show,* to *Cosby,* and is the author of several best-sellers.

Political comedian **Barry Crimmins's** CD is called *Kill the Messenger,* which he has also done on *Evening at the Improv.*

David Cross is cocreator and one of the stars of HBO's anarchistic sketch show, *Mr. Show.*

Billy Crystal is a director and actor of films that include *When Harry Met Sally* and *City Slickers,* and is host of HBO's "Comic Relief" and the Oscars.

d

Rodney Dangerfield, who has starred in the movies *Caddyshack, Back to School,* and improbably enough, Oliver Stone's film *Natural Born Killers,* won a Grammy for his comedy album *No Respect.*

Ellen DeGeneres was the star of ABC's *Ellen* and author of the best-selling *My Point . . . and I Do Have One.*

Sully Diaz has evolved from a South American soap-opera star into a comedy goddess.

Andy Dick is one of the stars of NBC's *NewsRadio.*

Jeannie Dietz has written jokes for Joan Rivers.

Bob Dubac is a comedian who also played the heartthrob on the soap opera *Loving.*

Mike Dugan has performed on *Evening at the Improv* and Showtime's *Comedy Club Network.*

Bil Dwyer has appeared on most of the defunct standup comedy shows, and has had guest starring roles on two of the hippest television shows, *The Larry Sanders Show* and *Ally McBeal.*

e

Bill Engvall has appeared on *The Tonight Show,* and was a cast member of *The Jeff Foxworthy Show.*

f

Jennifer Fairbanks has performed on UPN's *Vibe,* and is a member of the comedy troupe Fresh Meat and an award-winning San Francisco improv group.

Wayne Federman has appeared on *The Tonight Show* and MTV's *Half Hour Comedy Hour.*

Hugh Fink is a writer for *Saturday Night Live* and has appeared on Comedy Central's *Comedy Product* and MTV's *Half Hour Comedy Hour.*

Suzanne Flagge has appeared on the *Keenan Ivory Wayans Show.*

Jeff Foxworthy was the star of ABC's *The Jeff Foxworthy Show,* and was the best-selling author of *You Might Be a Redneck If . . .*

Jamie Foxx is the star of *The Jamie Foxx Show* on WBN.

Redd Foxx has been a stand-up comedian for over forty years. He was the star of the 1970s sitcom *Sanford and Son.*

Al Franken is the star of the sitcom *Lateline* and is the author of *Rush Limbaugh Is a Big Fat Idiot and Other Observations*.

g

Zach Galifianakis studied at the Royal Academy of Dramatic Arts in London, and is now a Los Angeles-based comedian. Go figure.

Gallagher is the giant prop comedian known for his numerous Showtime specials, often rerun on Comedy Central.

Billy Garan has appeared on Showtime's *Comedy on the Road* and their sitcom *Sherman Oaks,* as well as on A&E's *Evening at the Improv.*

Jeff Garlin regularly appears on the hit series, *Mad About You,* has starred in his very own HBO *Comedy Half Hour,* and also directed Denis Leary's special "Lock 'N Load."

Janeane Garofalo is the queen of the alternative comedians and an actress who has appeared in the films *Reality Bites* and *The Truth about Cats and Dogs,* as well as playing the booker on HBO's *The Larry Sanders Show.*

Geechy Guy has appeared on *Comic Strip Live* and *Evening at the Improv* and was a semi-finalist on *Star Search.*

Adele Givens has appeared on *Def Comedy Jam* and had her very own HBO *Comedy Half Hour.*

Todd Glass has become a veritable fixture on Comedy Central, appearing in a range of their shows from *Comic Cabana* to *Pulp Comics.*

Lisa Goich has opened for Tim Allen, Robert Goulet, and Paula Poundstone and appeared on *The Jenny McCarthy Show* on MTV.

Judy Gold has appeared on HBO's *Comic Relief,* was a cast member of the sitcom *All American Girl,* and is a producer of the *Rosie O'Donnell Show.*

Whoopi Goldberg is the Oscar-winning actress of the film *Ghost,* is cohost of HBO's *Comic Relief,* and has hosted the Oscars.

Bobcat Goldthwait plays the fuzzy bunny on the sitcom *Unhappily Ever After* and is the host of *Bobcat's Big Ass Show* on the FX network.

Mimi Gonzalez was one of Comedy Central's *Women Out Loud.*

Dana Gould is a cast member of the NBC sitcom *Working,* and has had two of his own one-man shows on Showtime.

Robin Greenspan has appeared on Comedy Central's *Out There in Hollywood.*

Michael Greer has guest-starred on Disney's *Dark Wing Duck,* and appeared in the movies *The Lonely Guy* and *The Rose.*

Dick Gregory was a ground-breaking black fifties comedian and civil rights activist.

David Allen Grier was one of the stars of *In Living Color* and has also been featured in the movie *Boomerang.*

Debi Gutierrez made her cable debut on Lifetime's *Girls Night Out,* and followed it up with Showtime's *Latino Laugh Festival.*

h

Rich Hall is a former *Saturday Night Live* cast member, who was also a comedy anchor on *Not Necessarily the News.*

Argus Hamilton is a political comedian who was a *Tonight Show* regular.

Rhonda Hansome is a comedian who has opened for James Brown, the Pointer Sisters, and Anita Baker.

Lacie Harmon is a Los Angeles-based comedian.

Brynn Harris is a Los Angeles-based comedian, and producer of the showcase "The Mix."

Alan Havey has appeared on the *David Letterman* show, and his own Showtime special.

Paulara R. Hawkins has done comedy at the Comedy Store, Steve Harvey's Comedy House in Dallas, and on *The Jenny Jones Show.*

Robert Hawkins has appeared on Showtime's *Full Frontal Comedy* and at the Montreal Just For Laughs Comedy Festival.

Susan Healy is a Los Angeles-based comedian.

Mitch Hedberg, winner of the Seattle Comedy Competition, has twice appeared on the *Late Show with David Letterman.*

Kevin Hench has appeared on NBC's *Friday Night Videos* and written comedy material for the ESPY Awards.

Rene Hicks was nominated for a 1998 American Comedy Award.

Charlie Hill is a comedian and Native American activist who has performed on *The Tonight Show.*

Vanessa Hollingshead has appeared on Comedy Central's *Tompkins Square Park,* A&E's *Evening at the Improv,* and Lifetime's *Girls Night Out.*

John Hope has performed comedy in forty-six states, one U.S. territory, Canada, and the Bahamas, and his writing has earned him a CableAce Award nomination.

Darlene Hunt has guest-starred on Comedy Central's *Comics on Delivery.*

Warren Hutcherson has starred in his own HBO *Half Hour Comedy* special, been featured at the Aspen Comedy Festival, and was a producer of the sitcom *Living Single.*

i

Dom Irrera hosted Showtime's *Full Frontal Comedy,* and has been nominated for a number of American Comedy Awards.

j

A.J. Jamal hosted Showtime's *Comedy from the Carribean,* and also appeared on *Comic Strip Live* and *Evening at the Improv.*

Jeffrey Jena has appeared on *Evening at the Improv,* Showtime's *Comedy Club Network,* and *Comic Strip Live.*

Richard Jeni has been rewarded for his comic fluidity with two CableAce and one American Comedy Awards.

Geri Jewell has appeared on *Girls Night Out, Comic Strip Live,* and was a recurring character on the sitcom *Facts of Life.*

Jake Johannsen starred in his own HBO *One Night Stand,* and was nominated for an American Comedy Award.

Jenny Jones is host of *The Jenny Jones Show.*

Heidi Joyce has been featured on Lifetime's *Girls Night Out,* and is the host of the Los Angeles showcase "Standup Comics Take a Stand Against Domestic Violence."

k

Kennedy Kasares is an L.A.–based comedian.

Jackie Kashian has appeared on A&E's *Comedy on the Road* and at HBO's U.S. Comedy Arts Festival.

Vanessa Kaufman has performed on Lifetime's *Girls Night Out.*

Sheila Kay has appeared on *Evening at the Improv,* Lifetime's *Girls Night Out,* and *Caroline's Comedy Hour.*

Lori Kaye has appeared on Lifetime's *Girls Night Out* and A&E's *Comedy from the Caribbean.*

Maura Kennedy has appeared on *Cybill,* is a recurring character on *Days of Our Lives,* and didn't *Win Ben Stein's Money.*

Tom Kenny is a cast member of HBO's *Mr. Show* and has been a host of *Friday Night Videos.*

Laura Kightlinger specialized in sublime sarcasm as the host of Comedy Central's *Stand Up, Stand Up,* and has been featured on *Saturday Night Special* and *Saturday Night Live.*

Craig Kilborn is the host of Comedy Central's *Daily Show.*

Karen Kilgariff has delivered on Comedy Central's *Comics on Delivery.*

Andy Kindler is the host of Animal Planet's *The Pet Shop,* has been one of HBO's *Young Comedians,* and has become a fixture on Comedy Central from *Dr. Katz* to *Comedy Product.*

Alan King is a classic comic from the fifties who has appeared on *The Tonight Show* and *The Ed Sullivan Show,* and performed in the movies *Just Tell Me What You Want* and *Memories of Me.*

Nosmo King is a comedian and cocreator of the Los Angeles showcase "Dreamland."

Dani Klein is both a comedian and an actor who recently worked with John Cleese in the remake of *The Out of Towners*.

Sue Kolinsky has performed on *The Tonight Show* and many other comedy shows.

Paul Krassner's CD, *We Have Ways of Making You Laugh*, was recently released on Mercury Records.

Bob Kubota has appeared on *Caroline's Comedy Hour*.

Cathy Ladman was the 1992 American Comedy Award-winning Best Female Standup of the Year, has racked up nine *Tonight Show* appearances, and plays a recurring character on *Caroline in the City*.

Steve Landesman was a popular sixties comedian and cast member of *Barney Miller*.

Beth Lapides created the Los Angeles showcase, "The Uncabaret" and its Comedy Central special, and has also appeared on *Politically Incorrect* and Comedy Central's *Women Aloud*.

Rocky LaPorte has appeared on *Caroline's Comedy Hour, Cheers,* and VH-1's *Standup Spotlight*.

Denis Leary is the star of a number of films, including *The Ref* and *Two If by Sea,* and star of his own HBO special "Lock 'N Load."

Carol Leifer was coproducer of NBC's *Seinfeld,* and was star of the series *Alright Already.*

Le Maire has appeared on Comedy Central's *Make Me Laugh* and has opened for Caroline Rhea.

Jay Leno is host of NBC's *The Tonight Show.*

David Letterman is host of CBS's *The Late Show.*

Cynthia Levin has starred in four very well-received one-woman shows, and performs regularly on the alternative circuit in Los Angeles.

In addition to his numerous HBO specials, **Richard Lewis** costarred on the sitcoms *Anything But Love* and *Hiller and Diller.*

Wendy Liebman is a *Tonight Show* regular, and has also appeared on *Late Night with David Letterman.*

Okay, she's not a comedian, but **Fran Liebowitz** is the incisively witty author of the recently rereleased *Metropolitan Life.*

Penelope Lombard was a host of *Friday Night Videos,* has appeared on Comedy Central's *Make Me Laugh,* and is one of the founders of the L.A. showcase "The Grrrl Genius Club."

George Lopez recently released his CD, *Alien Nation.*

Susie Loucks has appeared on *Evening at the Improv, Caroline's Comedy Hour,* and an impressive number of other comedy shows.

Mark Lundholm has taken his "twelve-step comedy" to comedy clubs and detox centers across the country.

Hellura Lyle is a Los Angeles–based comedian and a domestic violence peer counselor who performs in the showcase "Standup Comics Take a Stand Against Domestic Violence."

m

Mike MacDonald has starred in three Showtime and CBS specials including "Mike MacDonald: On Target."

Norm MacDonald starred in the comedy movie *Dirty Work,* and rumor has it that he was demoted from *Saturday Night Live's* "Weekend Update" by O.J. Simpson buddy and NBC executive Don Ohlmeyer for the O.J. joke we've printed here.

Kathleen Madigan won the 1996 American Comedy Award for Best Female Standup and starred in her very own HBO *Comedy Half Hour.*

Dexter Madison has appeared on *Evening at the Improv* and PBS's *Comedy Tonight.*

Bill Maher is host of ABC's *Politically Incorrect.*

Chris Mancini's work experience has ranged from being a spotter for *American Gladiators* to a writer for MTV, and he is also the creator of the Los Angeles showcase "The Alternative Comedy Nite."

Howie Mandel was a star of the series *St. Elsewhere*, the creator of his own cartoon show, *Bobby's World,* and the host of his own talk show.

Marilyn is a member of the L.A. comedy troupe The Hot and Spicy Mamitas.

Merrill Markoe was the head writer for the original *David Letterman* show, a reporter for *Alien Nation,* and is the author of Merrill Markoe's *Guide to Love.*

Bios

Steve Marmel is a CableAce–nominated writer for the Cartoon Network's *Cow and Chicken* and *Johnny Bravo* and appeared on Showtime's *Full Frontal Comedy* and Comedy Central's *Make Me Laugh.*

Mike Maron hosts the Microsoft Network weekly live cyber-cast, "This Is Not a Test."

Steve Martin has been the star of a number of films, from *The Jerk* to *L.A. Story* and *The Spanish Prisoner.*

Jackie Mason is a thirty-year comedy veteran and the star of several one-man Broadway shows.

Sabrina Matthews has been featured on Comedy Central's *Out There in Hollywood* and performed at the Montreal Just for Laughs Festival.

Jack Mayberry is a political comedian who has appeared on *The Tonight Show.*

Suli McCullough is coauthor of the book *150 Ways to Tell if You're Ghetto.*

Heather McDonald was a writer for the *Keenan Ivory Wayans Show.*

Mike McDonald recently appeared on *Just Shoot Me!*

Kristine McGaha has appeared on Showtime's *Full Frontal Comedy* and the syndicated series *Nightstand.*

Carlos Mencia was nominated for a CableAce award for his HBO *Comedy Half Hour.*

John Mendoza has appeared on *The Tonight Show* and one of Showtime's *Pair of Jokers.*

Felicia Michaels played a recurring character on ABC's *Full House,* was a *Star Search* winner, and was nominated for an American Comedy Award.

Cathryn Michon is a former writer for *Designing Women*, a current standup comedian, and cocreator of the Los Angeles showcase the "Grrrl Genius Club."

Beverly Mickins has been featured on Lifetime's *Girls Night Out.*

Bette Midler is the comedy diva who has appeared everywhere from *Beaches* to *The First Wives Club.*

Frank Miles has appeared everywhere from *Caroline's Comedy Hour* to *The Larry Sanders Show.*

Dennis Miller is the star of, natch, *The Dennis Miller Show* on HBO.

Larry Miller has starred in several HBO and Showtime specials, was a recurring character on *Mad About You,* and appeared in the movies *Pretty Woman* and *Necessary Roughness.*

Stephanie Miller survived her own *Stephanie Miller Show* on Fox to costar on an MSNBC talk show.

Jay Mohr has starred in several films, including *Jerry McGuire* and *Paulie.*

Tim Monahan is a member of the Little Tasty Cakes Los Angeles Comedy troupe, and has performed in comedy clubs across the country.

Carol Montgomery has appeared on *Evening at the Improv,* Showtime's *Comedy Club Network,* and *Girls Night Out.*

Lynda Montgomery has appeared on VH-1's *Spotlight,* and, she tells us, is "a regular performer on the Lavender Circuit."

Arthur Montmorency is a Los Angles–based comedian who has performed several one-man shows at HBO Workspace, including his "Scarboy."

Paul Mooney was a writer for Richard Pryor, has been featured on HBO nine times, and is father to the Mooney Twins.

Nancy Mura was host of *Fox Cubhouse,* and she has apppeared on *Evening at the Improv* and *Girls Night Out.*

After **Christy Murphy** became a finalist in Comedy Central's Don't Quit Your Day Job contest, she quit her day job.

Leslie Nesbitt says she's "a stand-up dame who won't go moxie on you," and she's contributed to Bill Maher's monologues for *Politically Incorrect* and performed on *Make Me Laugh.*

Taylor Negron was one of the cast of the sitcom *Hope and Gloria,* has appeared on *Evening at the Improv* and Comedy Central's "Uncabaret" special, and movies including *Punchline* and *The Last Boyscout.*

Bob Newhart is the comedian who has had several sitcoms named after him—for good reason—and most recently starred in *George and Leo.*

Diane Nichols was called "a Queen of Comedy" and "the heroine of the 9–5 crowd" by *Newsweek.*

Lydia Nicole has won a Youth in Film Inspiration Award for her work in the movie *Stand and Deliver.*

Susan Norfleet has been a *Tonight Show* regular, and recently appeared on *The Rosie O'Donnell Show* and *Ellen.*

O

Conan O'Brien is the host of NBC's *Late Night with Conan O'Brien.*

Bob Odenkirk is one-half of HBO's deconstructed skit show *Mr. Show,* and also played Larry's agent on the late, lamented *Larry Sanders Show.*

Cary Odes has performed on *Evening at the Improv,* Showtime's *Comedy Club Network,* and *Comic Strip Live.*

Rosie O'Donnell is host of the daytime talk show *The Rosie O'Donnell Show.*

Mary O'Halloran is an actress and comedian who has appeared in the movie *Housesitter.*

Dyana Ortelli is a Latino comedian and an actress who has been typecast straight down the line, starting with a maid on *Seinfeld.*

Bob Oshack is a Los Angeles–based comedian who performs at the Comedy Store.

Patton Oswalt has starred in his very own HBO *Comedy Central Half Hour,* has been featured on the Aspen Comedy Festival, and has written for *MAD TV* and *Austin Stories.*

Tamayo Otsuki has performed comedy on the Playboy Channel and appeared on *Evening at the Improv* and Showtime's *Comedy Club Network.*

Rick Overton was a writer for *The Dennis Miller Show* and has appeared on *Seinfeld* and in the movie *Mrs. Doubtfire.*

p

Tom Parks has been a regular on *The Tonight Show* and was a comedy anchor for *Not Necessarily the News.*

Pat Paulsen was a sixties comedian and star of the *Smothers Brothers Show,* who satirically ran for president for three decades.

Emo Philips has appeared on numerous HBO and Showtime specials, and is currently working on his own movies in England.

Monica Piper has had her own Showtime special "Only You, Monica" and has written for *Roseanne.*

Brenda Pontiff costarred on the sitcom *The Five Mrs. Buchanans* and has performed as a comedian at the Improvisation, the Comedy Store, and the Laugh Factory.

Brian Posehn is a cast member of HBO's *Mr. Show,* and has also appeared in the U.S. Comedy Arts Festival in Aspen.

Paula Poundstone is a veteran of numerous HBO appearances, including *Comic Relief* and "Paula Poundstone Goes to Harvard."

Paul Provenza starred on the last season of *Northern Exposure,* and has appeared in a number of HBO and Showtime comedy specials, including "The Incredible Man/Boy."

Robbie Printz is a Los Angeles–based comedian.

Greg Proops is one of the frightfully inventive stars of Comedy Central's *Whose Line Is It Anyway?*

Richard Pryor is a thirty-year film and TV veteran, including the ground-breaking seventies *Richard Pryor Show,* and the movie *Silver Streak.*

q

Colin Quinn is the anchor of "Weekend Update" on *Saturday Night Live.*

r

Georgia Ragsdale has appeared on Comedy Central's *Women Aloud* and in the PBS special "In the Life."

Michael Rasky was the featured comedian at the L.A. Gay Pride Festival and has performed at the Improv and the Comedy Store in Los Angeles.

Larry Reeb has appeared on Showtime's *Comedy Club All-Stars,* and A&E's *Evening at the Improv.*

Paul Reiser is the star of NBC's *Mad About You,* and author of the books *Couplehood* and *Parenthood.*

Caroline Rhea isn't a witch, but she plays one on TV, lovable Aunt Hilda on *Sabrina the Teenage Witch,* and she's also appeared in her own HBO special and on Comic Relief.

Joan Rivers is an actress, talk show host, and best-selling author.

Denise Munro Robb appeared on A&E's *Comedy on the Road.*

Robin Roberts was a writer/voice performer for the nationally syndicated radio show *Rick Dee's Weekly Top 40,* and is the creator of the Los Angeles showcase "Comedy by the Book."

Chris Rock is the star of HBO's *Chris Rock Show.*

Paul Rodriguez starred in the sitcom *AKA Pablo,* and on numerous HBO specials and *Comic Relief.*

Ray Romano is the fulcrum of CBS's *Everybody Loves Raymond.*

Roseanne was the star and a producer of ABC's *Roseanne.*

Jeffrey Ross was one of Comedy Central's *Pulp Comics.*

Patty Ross has appeared on Lifetime's *Girls Night Out.*

Rita Rudner has been featured on any number of comedy specials, including her own on HBO.

Tom Ryan has appeared on Showtime, A&E, and *Comedy Central* and he has written for ABC's *Politically Incorrect with Bill Maher.*

S

Bob Saget was the host of ABC's *America's Funniest Home Videos,* and the sitcom *Full House.*

Being ecology minded, we like to think of **Soupy Sales's** slap-happy performance style as recycled humor. If you're too young to have caught his fifties/sixties kiddie show, you can re-create the experience through his Rhino videos.

Mort Sahl was a ground-breaking fifties political comedian who appeared on *The Tonight Show.*

Betsy Salkind has been a staff writer for ABC's *Roseanne.*

Lowell Sanders has been featured on Showtime's *Full Frontal Comedy* and their *Comedy Club All Stars VII.*

Vance Sanders has written for Jay Leno and is a Los Angeles–based comedian and creator of the SCOOME Awards, noting the achievements of the Southern California Organization of Open Mikers.

Bios

Adam Sandler is a former cast member of NBC's *Saturday Night Live* and starred in the films *Billy Madison* and *Happy Gilmore.*

Drake Sather has appeared on *Late Night with David Letterman* and HBO's *Young Comedian Special,* and he is a sitcom writer.

Charisse Savarin has appeared on Fox TV's *Sunday Comics* and written jokes for Jay Leno.

Robert Schimmel's Warner Bros. CD is *Schimmel Comes Clean.*

Jerry Seinfeld was the star of NBC's *Seinfeld* and author of the best-selling *SeinLanguage.*

Garry Shandling was the star of HBO's *The Larry Sanders Show* and numerous other HBO specials.

Shang is a costar of *The Jamie Foxx Show* on WBN and has been featured in Best of the Fest on the U.S. Comedy Arts Festival on HBO.

Mark Shapiro was the winner of the Funniest Person in L.A. contest.

Craig Shoemaker is the host of VH-1's new trivia show, *My Generation,* and hosted ABC's hour-long special "Real Funny."

Will Shriner was a *Tonight Show* and *David Letterman* regular.

Laura Silverman is the voice of the sardonic receptionist Laura on Comedy Central's *Dr. Katz.*

Her sister, **Sarah Silverman,** has played a comedy writer on *Larry Sanders,* after being a comedy writer on *Saturday Night Live.*

Bios

Scott Silverman appeared on Comedy Central's *Out There 2*.

Sinbad was the host of the talk show *Vibe* and has starred in the film *House Guest*.

Carol Siskind has appeared on *Evening at the Improv, Comic Strip Live, Girls Night Out,* and innumerable other comedy specials.

Daryl Sivad was a cast member of the sitcom *The Naked Truth,* and has appeared on *The Tonight Show*.

Bobby Slayton's CD *Raging Bully* was recently released by Miramar Recordings, and he appeared in the HBO film *The Rat Pack* as Joey Bishop.

Bruce Smirnoff has appeared on nearly every cable comedy show extant, and took his one-man show *All I Have Is My Health and Today I Don't Feel So Good,* to the Montreal Just For Laughs Festival.

Bob Smith is one of the first out comedians to appear on TV and is the author of *Openly Bob*.

Margaret Smith was the winner of an American Comedy Award, and is a sitcom writer.

Tracy Smith has appeared on MTV's *Half Hour Comedy Hour,* and Lifetime's *Girls Night Out*.

Carrie Snow has appeared on at least a dozen of the cable comedy shows, and was a writer for *Roseanne*.

Former *Saturday Night Live* cast member **David Spade** now stars on the hit sitcom *Just Shoot Me!*

Spanky has appeared on *Evening at the Improv* and Showtime's *Comedy Club Network*.

Bios

Peter Spruyt is a standup comedian and coproducer of the Los Angeles showcase "Dreamland."

Jon Stewart hosted the former MTV show *The Jon Stewart Show*.

Jeff Stilson has appeared on the *David Letterman* show and has been featured in the fourteenth HBO *Young Comedians Show*.

Fred Stoller was a writer for *Seinfeld* and has appeared on *Caroline in the City*.

Pam Stone was a cast member of *Coach*, and recently made an appearance on *The Drew Carey Show*.

Jason Stuart has guest-starred on *The Drew Carey Show* and was featured in *Vegas Vacation* with Chevy Chase.

Lisa Sundstedt has been a featured performer in the Montreal Just for Laughs Festival, and a guest star in *Tracy Takes On*.

Glenn Super has appeared on *Evening at the Improv* and Showtime's *Comedy Club Network*.

Brad Stine has appeared on *Evening at the Improv* and *Comic Strip Live*.

Julia Sweeney was one of the cast of *Saturday Night Live*, and starred in her very own Broadway show, *God Said, "Ha!"*

t

Kim Tavares has appeared on BET and a Paul Rodriguez Showtime special.

Judy Tenuta has starred in her own HBO, Lifetime, and Showtime specials, and was a Grammy nominee for her comedy album.

Warren Thomas was featured on *Showtime's Comedy Club All Stars, Evening at the Improv,* and *Comic Strip Live.*

Scott Thompson, a former Kid in the Hall, also played Hank's Homo-American assistant on *The Larry Sanders Show.*

Christopher Titus, another comedy cable regular, also includes the cult classic *Killer Klowns from Outer Space* on his résumé.

Paul F. Tomkins was a writer/performer for HBO's *Mr. Show* and has appeared on the *Conan O'Brien Show.*

Lily Tomlin was an original cast member of *Laugh In,* starred in several films including *Nashville,* and most recently costarred on *Murphy Brown.*

Greg Travis has appeared on *Evening at the Improv,* Showtime's *Comedy Club Network,* and has made an appearance in several movies.

V

Cheril Vendetti has appeared on *Evening at the Improv, Girl's Night Out,* and played comedy clubs across the country.

Luda Vika has done all the TV shows that celebrate comedy tonality—*Comedy Compadres, Loco Slam, In Living Color.*

W

Don Ware has appeared on Showtime's *Comedy Club Network.*

George Wallace is a regular on both *The Tonight Show* and *David Letterman's Late Night,* and winner of an American Comedy Award.

Damon Wayans was the star and creator of the Fox series *In Living Color,* and starred in the movie *Mo' Money.*

Marlon Wayans is one of the stars of the *Wayans Brothers Show,* and, of course, one of the brothers.

Matt Weinhold was recently nominated for an award from the Academy of Interactive Arts and Sciences for the CD-ROM he wrote.

Lotus Weinstock was a beloved Los Angeles comedian whose comedy career spanned three decades, from her engagement to Lenny Bruce to appearances on *The Tonight Show, Evening at the Improv,* Lifetime's *Girls Night Out,* and her extensive charity work.

Mercedes Wence is a L.A.–based comedian.

Sheila Wenz has appeared on Lifetime, A&E, and Comedy Central.

Dan Whitney has appeared on Comedy Central and VH-1, and his *Larry the Cable Guy* is played in eighteen daily radio markets.

Penny Wiggins has appeared on *Evening at the Improv* and is the producer of the Los Angeles show "Sirens of Satire."

Harland Williams was the toasted star of the movies *Half-Baked* and *Rocket Man* and his very own HBO *Half Hour Comedy.*

Robin Williams received an Academy Award for *Good Will Hunting* and is the Academy Award–nominated star of *Mrs. Doubtfire* and *Flubber,* and star of the former ABC sitcom *Mork and Mindy* and a cohost of HBO's *Comic Relief.*

Dan Wilson has appeared on *Evening at the Improv* and MTV's *Half Hour Comedy Hour.*

Gary Wilson is a writer for *Cow and Chicken,* the animated series, and has performed on *Make Me Laugh.*

Jane Edith Wilson has appeared on Comedy Central's *Make Me Laugh* and appeared on *Seinfeld.*

Lizz Winstead was the creator and a star of the Comedy Channel's *Daily Show.*

Anita Wise has appeared on *The Tonight Show* and at the Just for Laughs Festival in Montreal.

Dennis Wolfberg was a beloved eighties comedian who was a *Tonight Show* regular, and was a cast member of the TV series *Quantum Leap.*

Jackie Wollner is the producer of the Los Angeles "Head On Comedy" showcase and a finalist in the prestigious San Francisco Comedy Competition.

Steven Wright has appeared on numerous HBO specials, was a recurring cast member of *Mad About You,* and was nominated for an Oscar for Best Short Film.

Robert Wuhl is the star of HBO's sitcom *Arliss.*

y

Pamela Yager has appeared on *Saturday Night Live* and Comedy Central's *Stand Up, Stand Up.*

Henny Youngman was a fifty-year comedy veteran best known for his one-liners such as, "Take my wife . . . please."

z

Bob Zany was a semifinalist on *Star Search,* has been featured on Rodney Dangerfield's "Really Big Show" HBO Special, and appeared on *The Tonight Show.*